RENEWING AMERICA'S PROGRESS

RENEWING AMERICA'S
_____PROGRESS

A Positive Solution to School Reform

FREDRIC H. GENCK

New York
Westport, Connecticut
London

Library of Congress Cataloging-in-Publication Data

Genck, Fredric H.
  Renewing America's progress : a positive solution to school reform
/ Fredric H. Genck.
     p.   cm.
  Includes bibliographical references and index.
  ISBN 0-275-93651-1 (alk. paper)
  1. School management and organization—United States. 2. School
improvement programs—United States.   I. Title.
LB2801.A2G46   1991
371.2'00973—dc20   91-16658

British Library Cataloguing in Publication Data is available.

Library of Congress Catalog Card Number: 91-16658
ISBN: 0-275-93651-1

First published in 1991

Praeger Publishers, One Madison Avenue, New York, NY 10010
An imprint of Greenwood Publishing Group, Inc.

Printed in the United States of America

∞™

The paper used in this book complies with the
Permanent Paper Standard issued by the National
Information Standards Organization (Z39.48-1984).

10 9 8 7 6 5 4 3 2 1

Contents

Exhibits and Figures

EXHIBITS

FIGURES

Preface

Successful foreign competition is challenging America economically, and a possibly permanent underclass is causing continued urban crisis. The problem is not students, teachers, parents, or even drugs—but whether our schools and other public services are well managed and performing successfully. The solution is not welfare, prisons, deficits, or federal troops—but effective schools and public services, through the application of management that made America's national democracy, agriculture, and industry models for the rest of the world.

The public management revolution beginning in schools is the foundation we need for America's future. Here is a positive solution to drive forward America's progress and success into the twenty-first century—with improved school performance. To reduce school failure and urban decline, eliminate national deficits and the underclass, support civil rights and urban renewal, we need more than well-managed businesses and farms. We must also have well-managed public services. Public service reform is as important for our future as the American Revolution and the agricultural and industrial revolutions that followed it were for our history; it is as exciting as the democratic revolutions now reaching Eastern Europe and the agricultural and industrial revolutions still ahead for underdeveloped countries around the world.

This is the first generation to witness the potential end of America's progress and success. Positive school reform—the public management revolution beginning in America's schools—is the solution. The system of participative and results-oriented management described in this book draws on the best of America's traditions—our history of democratic, pragmatic, and progressive ideas leading to improved performance of the organizations that serve us—first in democracy, agriculture, and industry, and now in schools and public services. The purpose is to renew the American dream and to solve the urban crisis and declining school performance.

The three-year head start being achieved by teachers and students in districts using this system proves that America's schools can succeed in urban as well as suburban and rural communities. These achievements are setting new standards for expectations that can and should be applied to every school in America—by every citizen.

THE SYSTEM

Described and documented in this book is a complete system of participative management with board accountability and performance measures that is based on 15 years of research and experience in schools and districts across the country. The system is implemented through teamwork, participation, and accountability at three levels—boards, administrators, and teachers:

1. *Governance*—Participative and accountable policies and leadership for teamwork and success
2. *Management*—Positive planning, organization, evaluation, and compensation
3. *Performance*—Outside audit of learning and satisfaction to justify funding and salaries.

Results add three years of learning to eight years in school, plus higher satisfaction, confidence, morale, and cost-effectiveness.

AUDIENCE

This book is addressed to citizens *and* educators—those who receive school services and those who provide them:

• Every parent, student, and taxpayer concerned about the quality of America's schools
• Every teacher, administrator, and board member who wants to give America the quality schools we need for our future.

Only a system that involves and satisfies both groups can succeed.

Baby boomers now in their years of social responsibility, as well as young professionals and older Americans concerned about schools, need a practical, positive guide so their interest and concern can be constructive. Teachers, freed from traditional authoritarian school administration through unions, now are ready for participative and results-oriented management, in order to achieve good performance and to justify funding for good schools and fair salaries.

With the Cold War winding down, America's attention is returning to progressive reform, still unfinished for public services. The 1990s already show declining interest in self-help and rising concern with community and environment. Newspaper headlines, magazine covers, and television specials have made us concerned about school problems and the urban crisis. Now we need a positive solution.

RESULTS

This book proves that America's students and teachers can succeed. The potential for improving performance is dramatic. The message is one of hope and success. Actual results in pilot districts implementing this system included more learning, satisfaction, confidence, morale, teamwork, and accountability. This system of participative, results-oriented management—based on my work with thousands of board members, administrators, and teachers—results in the following:

- Improved student learning—a three-year head start
- Increased public confidence, parent satisfaction, staff morale, and teamwork, with fair evaluation and accountability
- Satisfied taxpayers, convinced that they are getting their money's worth and that funding for good schools and fair salaries is justified
- The better schools we need for America's future.

I have used my experience as a Harvard MBA, international management consultant, teacher, and school board member to detail the following in this book:

- A complete system of policies, plans, and measures—with implementation steps, forms, and procedures
- Application and results in schools and districts across the country
- Mounting evidence of improved performance
- Implementation plans for performance measures, the supporting management system, and board policies.

Specific practical examples include reports of performance improvements; management plans for organization, evaluation, and compensation; and criteria and procedures to evaluate the board, superintendent, administrators, and teachers.

The book's purpose is to support you in making a personal contribution to the public management revolution beginning in America's schools, strengthening local democracy and improving school performance.

Following this preface are four exhibits:

- The governance-management-performance system, linking board and staff, purpose and performance, people and results
- Three recent theories of school management leading to the management system in this book
- Profiles of four successful leaders to illustrate the management system
- A brief explanation of growth rates to help you understand references to improved performance.

Exhibit 1
Three Steps for Effective Schools

This three-part governance-management-performance system replaces traditional authoritarian administration, the conflict of recent years, and the old policy/administration model.

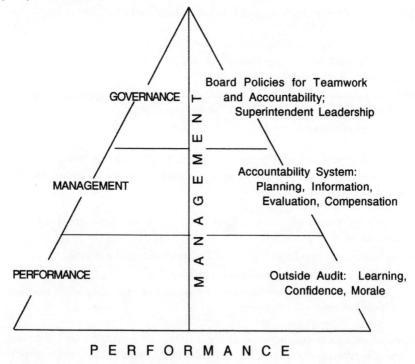

Results include improved performance; humane and participative relationships; an upward spiral of positive reinforcement; learning, confidence, morale, teamwork, and accountability.

Exhibit 2
ABCs of School Management

This is the transition from traditional authoritarian school administration and the adversarial relationships and conflict of recent years to participative and results-oriented management that is causing dramatic performance improvements in America's schools, cities, and other public services.

THEORY A	THEORY B	THEORY C
Phase I	Phase II	Phase III
1960s and before	1970s and 1980s	1990s
Traditional Authoritarian Administration	**Adversarial Relationships And Conflict**	**Participative Results-Oriented Management**
Informal, Undocumented, Back of the Envelope	Legalistic, Bureaucratic, Frightening, Confusing	Communication, Teamwork, and Success
Heavy Authority or Virtually Unmanaged	Declining Performance and Confidence	Democratic Governance, Participative Management, Performance Measures

Exhibit 3
Successful School Leaders

1. *Build Teamwork:* Don Skidmore, superintendent in the small rural community of Antioch, starts his day by having coffee with other residents at 6 a.m. in the local coffee shop. He talks with teachers to make sure their concerns are answered, replacing conflict with teamwork. He has succeeded in raising learning from average to superior.

2. *Set High Expectations:* Dorothy Boyd, superintendent in Hazel Crest, is coaching her principals on how to evaluate teachers; to encourge and retain those who are effective, and do something about those who are not. She has doubled student learning in a racially mixed community near the central city.

3. *Measure Results:* Charles Thomas, superintendent in the urban factory town of North Chicago, analyzes test scores to make sure each student is achieving

a full year's growth for a year in school. As a result of his leadership, student learning has doubled.

4. *Reward Good Performance:* Al Klingenberg is superintendent in prosperous suburban Lake Forest. A down-to-earth person in an upscale community, he has an unusual ability to convey a supportive attitude to other people. His standards and expectations are equally obvious. The combination is powerful. (See Chapter 2 for details.)

Exhibit 4
Growth Rates

This brief explanation is to provide you with a preliminary understanding of performance measures noted throughout the book. America's standardized achievement tests are a useful indicator of basic skills achievement by students. However, the scores are more a reflection of community income levels than of school performance. The best indicator is growth rates, also called annual gains or value added. For example, subtracting last year's fourth grade score from this year's fifth grade score measures how much progress students have made in one year. The national norm is a year of growth for a year in school (ten months using the school year).

The following are examples of the range of results:

- Three urban communities doubled growth rates, from six to twelve months per year.
- Two suburban districts added two years of growth to eight years in school.
- The highest district growth rate I have observed is a year and a half. The lowest is half a year.
- For individual schools and grades I have seen growth rates as high as two years. The lowest is zero.

Of course you also need other indicators, such as surveys of parent, teacher, and student satisfaction, and room for judgment. But if you had to choose one measure, growth rates would be a good choice.

Acknowledgments

Alfred Kahn, head of the Economics Department when I was a student at Cornell University (and later Jimmy Carter's inflation fighter and a leader in deregulation of industry) first helped me to understand the economic impacts of business and public policy.

Kenneth Andrews, who taught the business policy course when I was at the Harvard Business School, helped me to understand strategy and organization, and has since encouraged me to carry on in a public management direction.

Jim Allen, a founder of Booz, Allen & Hamilton, helped me move into public management. While serving as his assistant, I helped plan the School of Management at Northwestern University. John Barr and Ralph Westfall, dean and associate dean at what was Northwestern's Business School and is now the Graduate School of Management, also helped.

Peter Warner gave me the opportunity to practice in a smaller setting, essential to the work I have done with schools. And he provided encouragement without which I would not have gotten this far.

Al Klingenberg, superintendent in Lake Forest, Illinois, School District 67 (and coauthor with me of *Effective Schools Through Effective Management*), helped to conceive and apply the school management model described in this book.

Jerry Glaub and Hal Seamon of the Illinois Association of School Boards encouraged me and published my first book, *Effective Schools*. National associations—school boards, administrators, and PTA—have also been helpful.

David Wiley, dean of Northwestern's School of Education and Social Policy, helped me develop the school management case study course.

My friends in Phi Delta Kappa at Northwestern and elsewhere have lent insight to my understanding of teachers. I especially thank Jean Damisch, Nina Koelpin, David Whiting, Pat Hastings, Joe Boyd, and Dolores Solovy, who is also founder and head of the Kohl Teacher Center.

My clients in schools and districts across the country—thousands of superintendents, administrators, principals, teachers, parents, students, and taxpayers—helped to build the model.

All four of my children—Lauren, Fredric, Jennifer, and Ginger—have helped in editing this book and in many other ways.

Pattie Cichocki, Susan Walters, and Jean Charpentier managed the office, lent cheerful support, and produced the written word.

My colleagues at Booz, Allen & Hamilton, friends and advisers of the Institute, and the faculty at Northwestern's School of Education and Social Policy and Graduate School of Management have contributed ideas, discussion, and friendship.

My clients in business, government, and education in the United States and Europe since 1964 have given me an opportunity to develop, implement, and observe in practice the results of my ideas about management. It was especially helpful to work for American universities during the turbulent 1960s, and to have the opportunity to reorganize two local governments in England.

I am grateful to you all.

I

Overview: People and Results

Progress and Success: A Citizen's Guide

My purpose in writing this book is to enable every citizen—every parent, teacher, and taxpayer—to evaluate and improve his or her local schools, using my 25 years of management consulting experience to help you do so. This book contains everything you need to know, a complete do-it-yourself kit, to evaluate and improve your schools.

Democracy requires that citizens evaluate public services. In schools, this means that parents should be sure that they and their children are well served, taxpayers should be sure they are getting their money's worth, and teachers need to be able to reassure the public (and themselves) that good results justify budgets and salaries.

Everyone involved in schools—teachers, administrators, board members, other staff, taxpayers, parents, and students—needs a concept of school governance, management, and performance. This will help you organize your own commonsense perceptions and experience into effective action for improvement. You will have some idea of how to measure your school's performance; how to find out whether your school has a positive, supportive, participative, results-oriented management process or traditional authoritarian school administration; and how to see if your school board is setting policies of teamwork and success instead of the adversarial relationships, conflict, and decline into which many American school districts have fallen in the past few decades.

This book contains a practical, tested, proven system of governance, management, and performance—a complete system of performance measures, participative management, and accountable boards that is already beginning a management revolution in American's public services. As a result, some schools are outperforming their neighbors, and their own history, by as much as two to one. This system can achieve the same productivity improvements for education that America has accomplished in agriculture and industry. It will extend to teachers the same freedom with responsibility promised to citizens by the American Revolution. To do so, it must be applied more widely than it has been to date.

Use this book to make sure the public management revolution has reached your school—for good performance in student learning, public confidence, parent satisfaction, teacher morale, cost-effectiveness, teamwork, and accountability. Use it to measure and improve your school, to see if you are getting your money's worth, to make sure your school is good enough for your child, to apply these concepts to other public services, to give something back to your community, and to participate fully in the governance and management of your schools as a board member, administrator, teacher, or other staff member.

AMERICA'S PROGRESS AND SUCCESS

The urban and educational problems of America are our most serious moral failures of the twentieth century. The end of our national progress and success is being caused by school failure and urban decline. Poorly performing public schools in our cities are leading to the decline of America, saddling our nation with a frightening underdeveloped country in every American big city. Welfare, prisons, deficit spending, even federal troops have failed to solve the problem. Good schools are the only solution.

This tested, proven system of measuring, managing, and governing leads to good school performance: a solid foundation for America's continued progress and success; a participative and results-oriented approach satisfying to both teachers and parents. Examples describe and document successful schools and substantial performance improvements in urban, suburban, and rural communities.

WHO CAN HELP?

Every American should be interested in the message of this book, which is addressed to citizens in every community.

Baby boomers have reached an age of readiness for community involvement. Now in their years of social responsibility, they need a practical, positive guide so their energy can be used productively to solve America's problems. They need not feel helpless and confused about their local schools; they can use this book to channel anger, fear, and guilt into something constructive—correcting the public school failure that is causing the urban crisis and, potentially, America's national decline.

Young professionals, anxious about the education of their children, are ready to apply the same expectations for performance and results to public services that they experience in their employment. Now that 72 percent of Americans are employed in managerial, professional, or service jobs (compared with 3 percent on farms and 25 percent in industry), most people have a personal understanding of and interest in performance and management standards for public services.

Older Americans are often angry about taxes and worried about school quality. They have the time and the interest to read and apply performance and management standards. This book gives performance measures to be sure taxpayers are getting their money's worth, with management techniques and governance policies to improve the return on their tax investment.

America is returning to the unfinished agenda of domestic reform, successful shortly after the turn of the century in agriculture and industry but never fully completed with respect to public services. The "me" generation of the 1980s is giving way to concern for community and environment in the 1990s. Mounting evidence of the need for productivity improvements in education, health care, and government services has focused attention on these critical aspects of our society.

No one has more to gain from well-managed schools than teachers: moving managing closer to teaching, improving performance, proving that a good job is being done, justifying funding and salaries, and replacing traditional authoritarian administration with modern participative and results-oriented management.

Most parents are too busy—both parents work, or the family has a single parent—but only a few are needed to apply these standards to schools. Of course they lack the time to invent the standards, let alone to measure and manage school directly. Now that these policies, techniques, and measures have been tested and proven, their application does not need to take a lot of time; only a few people in each community are needed to get the process started.

Americans increasingly recognize that education is the axial function of a postindustrial society. Services, most of them public, are as important to our economic health today as agriculture and industry, which, through their productivity, have shrunk to a relatively small percentage of our economy.

SELF-HELP IS NOT ENOUGH

We need effective public services, too. Americans must extend their interest in self-help to community and environment in addition to personal health, career, and money. Schools are an issue on which all Americans can agree, one we must solve if our country is to prosper and succeed. In a democracy expectations determine the quality of public services. You can contribute by holding your schools accountable to the standards of governance, management, and performance in this book.

Positive, practical local school reform, using the plan documented in this book, will accomplish the following:

- Fulfill civil rights by adding economic competitiveness to equal opportunity
- Restart America's social progress by solving the urban crisis and reducing the underclass
- Renew America's economic success in a global society of information and services.

SUCCESSFUL EXPERIENCE—EVERY SCHOOL AND STUDENT CAN SUCCEED

More talk about problems is not enough. We need solutions: positive, practical answers tested and proven to turn around the performance of our public schools—pragmatic measures, successful management plans, governance standards we can apply to our own school boards and superintendents—to evaluate and improve our schools. This is not just another complaint, but instead a positive solution documented through 15 years of practical experience in hundreds of schools and districts across the country, developing and successfully applying a measurement and management system that produces good results, even in urban schools.

I will describe the history that led to the crisis, and the people who are helping to solve it. Anecdotes and real-life success stories prove that every American school and student can succeed. Outside audit reports document results. Some of these schools have turned around performance from the levels of our worst central city schools to learning rates equal to those in the best suburbs.

Some criticisms of American education imply that everything is failing. Some things have failed, but not everything. Surveys and test data analysis prove that some schools and districts, including those in urban communities, are successful. How have these excellent schools done it? The difference between high and low performance is management. High-performance districts answer "yes" to these questions.

- Are results measured?
- Are teachers and administrators evaluated?
- Is the board accountable?

To solve the problem when performance is not up to par, we need to apply techniques proved in districts that are already doing well: the board policies, management techniques, and performance measures that make the difference between success and failure.

A PROVEN SOLUTION

There are three components needed for success:

- *Performance measures*—To prove when a good job is being done, and to raise learning and satisfaction
- *Management plans*—Linking pay to performance—with recognition, reward, fair evaluation, and positive support
- *Governance policies*—For teamwork and accountability.

These three steps result in improved learning, confidence, and morale—and therefore provide a solid foundation for America's renewed economic success and social progress.

STOP BLAMING TEACHERS AND FIX THE SYSTEM

There is no need to blame anyone—not teachers, often overworked and underappreciated, or parents and students, sometimes victims of the system. Perhaps this puts it too strongly, but America's teachers have made the same mistake as the peasant in an underdeveloped country trying to run faster behind the ox and plow. Productivity is usually not improved by working harder—only by working smarter. A system of measurement and management is needed, not blaming teachers for problems they did not create and cannot solve. The guilty are not teachers, parents, or students, but passive citizens who stand by and watch our cities decline when the management and measurement techniques needed to turn around our schools and save our cities are available, tested, and proven.

Other public services are important, too—housing and social services, for example. But schools are the most positive, practical, and cost-effective solution to the urban crisis, the single most important investment we can make in America's future. It is not students, families, teachers, or even drugs that are causing our problem—it is the way schools are managed. America's urban schools have failed to change in the face of changing requirements, and this has caused the decline of American cities, as well as the decline of the American Dream.

THE SOLUTION: MEASURE PERFORMANCE

Governors, business leaders, and others have recognized the problem of poor school performance. But no one has clearly specified a proven and practical solution that the people can understand and apply. Measuring performance is the answer to America's school crisis. This is no more difficult than changing a tire on your car so you can continue your journey. The journey is America's continued social and economic progress. The flat tire is traditional authoritarian school administration, undermined, and rightly so, by teacher unions. This tradition has been replaced by an era of conflict leading to more assertive school boards and unmanaged schools, rather than by new management that meets the requirements of schools today.

The solution lies in the comprehensive, tested, proven system of board policies, management plans, and performance measures in this book. Examples and results focus on three specific action steps:

• Measure school results, starting at the bottom with student learning and parent and teacher satisfaction.

• Build a participative and results-oriented management system to replace traditional authoritarian school administration.

• Replace traditional "rubber stamp" school boards, and the conflict of recent years, with teamwork and accountability.

A PARTICIPATIVE AND RESULTS-ORIENTED SYSTEM

This is a simple three-step system of governance, management, and performance that anyone can understand and apply. Board policies for teamwork and accountability replace traditional "rubber stamp" school boards that took orders from all-powerful superintendents. The management system connects board and staff with positive support for teachers and administrators and a fair, effective system of planning, information, evaluation, and compensation—to implement policies of teamwork and accountability. Most important, a third level is added to the traditional American dichotomy between policy and administration in public affairs: measuring performance. The formula is

$$\frac{\text{Learning} \times \text{Confidence} \times \text{Morale}}{\text{Cost}}$$

This formula uses practical, proven measures for learning and satisfaction by analyzing test scores and surveying parents and teachers.

GROWTH RATES

We need pragmatic measures for schools like those which led to America's success in agriculture and industry. A year's growth for a year in school is a simple standard that anyone can apply and every school can achieve—as easy as miles per gallon, earnings per share, or yield per acre. You would not invest your money in a company that did not prove its growth and profit in an audited financial statement. This book shows how you can apply the same kind of standards to public services, starting with schools.

I will share with you the results of applying these measures, with evidence that performance often differs by as much as two to one, even in similar neighboring communities. These standards must be applied by someone. Americans who have stood up and watched our cities decline and our schools fail must now help to solve these problems. Of course, good results cannot be achieved overnight. This book is your guide to help apply, with a little well-directed effort, measures of school performance and standards of management.

GOOD SCHOOLS MEAN URBAN SUCCESS

Each new generation faces a window of opportunity to solve the urban crisis, starting from the time they begin school. Then, once they reach puberty, the distractions of modern life lead to high dropout rates for those who cannot read and write, and for many of these, a lifetime of crime, drugs, unemployment, and welfare.

Three urban communities have doubled the growth rate of student learning by using my system. They have improved dramatically from the low single-digit growth rate levels found in many big city schools to double-digit growth rates equal to or better than suburban schools. And they have achieved additional improvements in confidence, satisfaction, morale, teamwork, and accountability. I have seen increases of at least 20 to 30 percent in growth rates of student learning in every community that has applied this system. The pattern has been replicated in hundreds of districts across the country, from Apache Junction, Arizona, to Williamsburg, Virginia. These improvements are accomplished by applying measurement and management techniques that have been demonstrated to be successful. The system has not only been tested and proven but also practiced and endorsed by management experts, leading educators, and representatives of teachers, administrators, and school boards.

GOOD SCHOOLS BENEFIT EVERYONE

Solving the urban crisis, underclass, welfare, crime, unemployment, and deficit problems—and financing our national economic prosperity—are important potential contributions of the solution described in this book. The system will improve school performance in upscale and middle-class suburbs, small towns and rural areas, as well as cities. Ten districts representing various social and economic circumstances implemented the system in the 1970s and 1980s. I have monitored their performance. The results: these schools raised learning by an average of 37 percent. The message is important everywhere, especially in cities where school failure and the urban crisis threaten. Even citizens whose local schools are not failing can use these techniques to improve performance dramatically. This school management model can be used to get America back on the course of prosperity and success instead of conflict and decline.

RENEWED AMERICAN PROGRESS AND SUCCESS

Now is the time to reach out to the schools with this message of hope and success—a positive solution to school failure, urban crisis, and economic decline, a proven system to evaluate and improve the schools. Higher national standards and expectations for school performance and management will renew America's progress and success, and raise the achievements and capabilities of our children. This will make America more competitive in the world economy; renew civil rights progress; raise property values; eliminate the underclass; reduce the need for (and cost of) prisons, welfare, unemployment, and social services; solve the dilemma of federal deficits; and take a first step toward practical, positive reform of all public services.

PUBLIC MANAGEMENT REVOLUTION

Well-managed public services, as well as businesses and farms, are needed to get America moving again. The public management revolution beginning in schools must be extended to every public service if America is to prosper in the twenty-first century. In a global information and service economy, effective management of services, most of them public, is an important requirement for national progress and success. The concept of public management stressing people and results was introduced in my first book, *Effective Schools* (written with Dr. Allen J. Klingenberg), which helped to establish the need for and direction of school reform across the country. A second book, *Improving School Performance*, detailed the management system developed from my consulting, research, and teaching. A series of twelve do-it-yourself implementation handbooks for administrators (the School Management Model series) provided implementation examples, results, forms, and procedures.

This book takes the concept a step further, updating the results of my research, showing how the behavioral sciences, participative management, the scientific method, and the measuring of results can be applied in schools and other public services. Details of plans and results are in a separate series of handbooks (the School Board Accountability series).

2

Exemplary School Leaders: Lessons from America's Best-Managed Schools

The school superintendents described in this chapter are a microcosm of our nation in rural, urban, and suburban areas; the children in their schools are black and white, rich and poor. Their success proves that the governance-management-performance system can be applied effectively, that teachers really do make a difference, and that all children can achieve greater success.

What do these exemplary school leaders have in common? It is a style that pays attention to people, listens to "customers" and staff, and responds—leadership in the best sense of the word. In schools this translates into the following:

- Communication, teamwork, trust, and confidence among board and staff—with accountability and responsiveness to parents, students, and taxpayers
- Administrative responsibility for performance, with evaluation and compensation to match
- A participative, open style of management that is currently used in business
- Performance information to prove where a good job is being done and to identify improvement opportunities, analyzing and using this information to improve performance—and caring enough about performance to bother with the information and analysis
- Recognition and reward for teachers and other staff members, good salaries based on good performance, evaluation that is fair and effective, support for development and improvement instead of conflict and fragmentation

Listing these steps is easy. Implementing them is challenging. Communication means responding if someone is concerned. Evaluation means that sometimes a teacher has to be fired, counseled to enter another field, or encouraged to change in some basic way. Information means that something must be done when performance is not up to par. Recognition and reward require discriminating between good performers and the rest.

The search for excellence is not easy, but the results in schools, as in other kinds of organizations, are stunning. Three of the school districts involved in a pilot program to apply the governance-management-performance system have doubled student learning. Ten pilot districts have raised learning by 37 percent. Some of the districts with the greatest performance improvements were achieving no more than some of our poorest inner city schools in similar circumstances when they started, while others showed improvement even though they started from above-average levels.

These districts are characterized by teamwork, trust, and confidence in staff relations instead of conflict, adversarial relationships, and fragmentation. The public is confident that schools are performing well. Taxpayers feel they are getting their money's worth. Parents are satisfied with the progress of their children. Most of these districts are achieving these results without spending more than others; in some cases educational costs are actually less. These are not just wealthy suburban communities. Successful examples range from rural to urban areas and include every kind of social and economic background.

TEAMWORK

Don Skidmore has been superintendent in Antioch, a small town near a lakeside resort area, for ten years. Before he came, the district had several superintendents in a few years. Board and staff were not on speaking terms. Strikes occurred almost every year. The academic program was disorganized. Learning was about average.

Don can be found every morning at 6 A.M. having coffee with other residents in the local coffee shop. You could easily mistake him for a farmer or a truck driver. As a model of how integrity and communication can turn a school district around, he is exemplary. Listening to parents and teachers and responding to their concerns and problems builds the kind of teamwork, trust, and confidence that is a common feature of successful school districts. Simple problems—such as not enough supplies, a pothole in the playground, or a sticky drawer—are solved. This allows teachers to concentrate on teaching without worrying about shortages or repairs that impeded their performance. The techniques may seem simple and commonplace, but they are essential. Coupled with other features of the accountability system, they can have a tremendous positive impact on performance. Just consider how much more helpful and supportive this is to teachers than siphoning off energy into strikes, bargaining, and adversarial relationships.

The most notable thing about the improvements in Antioch is that school performance before the turnaround seemed adequate for the level of intelligence indicated by test scores. Had Don accepted this common indicator of adequate performance when he became superintendent, it is unlikely that much would have changed. But he did not. In addition to settling down relationships and building trust and confidence, Don went to work organizing the curriculum and measuring results. Consequently, percentiles of achievement for the eighth grade rose from 55 percent to 69 percent during the first four years. Grade equivalents increased from 9.6 to 11.0. Annual growth is now averaging 15 months per year, compared with a national average of 10. Remarkably, the improvement in achievement is raising the indicated intelligence scores of students. In a pattern I have seen repeated in other districts, students' actual achievements are substantially exceeding what would be expected from their indicated intelligence at the first grade level; the intelligence scores rise as children move through the grades.

SUPPORT STAFF

Dorothy Boyd, superintendent in urban Hazel Crest, coaches her principals on how to evaluate teachers, encourage and retain those who are effective, and do something about those who are not. She has doubled student learning in a racially mixed community near the central city. Hazel Crest is an urban community adversely affected by the declining steel industry and the stress and strain of racial conflict growing out of historic patterns of segregation. Straddling a traditional racial boundary line, it is about half black and half white. The school district was forced to integrate by the state in the 1970s.

Before Dorothy's promotion to superintendent in Hazel Crest, she spent ten years as a principal in the same district. She is a hardworking black woman who has high expectations for everyone. You would not want to be the slow student in her classroom. These high standards are not without a stressful effect, especially on some of the older teachers in the district. Not only does Dorothy train principals, she holds them responsible for performance, with documented teacher responsibilities and the expectation of good results. Student achievement scores have improved throughout the 1980s, with a big jump during the first few years after Dorothy became superintendent. Growth rates averaged 8 months per year in the early 1970s, 10 to 12 months per year in the late 1970s, and more recently as high as 16 months per year. The single most important indicator of output suggests that district productivity has doubled, and that taxpayers are getting more than the national averages for their tax dollars. Another indicator of good performance, percentiles of achievement, averaged 73 percent for 1986–87, compared with a national average of 50 percent. Second grade IQ scores in Hazel Crest were only 90, substantially below the national average. This district is overachieving.

MEASURE RESULTS

Charles Thomas, superintendent in North Chicago, analyzes test scores to make sure that each child is achieving a full year's growth for each year in school. As a result of his leadership, student learning there almost doubled during the 1980s.

A football player at Wisconsin, Charles went on to get his master's and Ph.D. at Northwestern University. He was a teacher and administrator in one district, then served as a staff member in the State Office of Education. His leadership style makes board confidence seem natural; however, those who know the area understand that the community is divided. Many taxpayers are older, white, of Eastern European ethnic background, and have no children in school; parents of students are mostly younger, black, many of them on welfare and unemployed. Constant turnover occasioned by the local naval base makes Charles's job even more difficult.

North Chicago is an urban industrial community where the problems of smokestack industries are evidenced by closed stores and factories. Heavy industry still predominates, with all the usual problems. The district is one of the least affluent and lowest-spending in its county. Nevertheless, student learning in North Chicago showed dramatic improvement during the 1980s, with average annual months of growth doubling from six to twelve per year, compared with a national average of ten. Progress occurred in the first few years at the lower grade levels, but not at the junior high level. Careful monitoring of improvements motivated the reorganization back to K–8 buildings and closing the junior high school. North Chicago has been a leader in decentralizing the junior high school back to elementary buildings. Student learning has improved as a result. But most exciting is the ability of teachers to know individual students well, to spend virtually the full day with them, to have them in a school where they are known to other teachers and students, thus offsetting the fragmentation so common in the lives of young people today.

Charles Thomas's expectation that every student can be successful and his willingness to hold teachers and administrators accountable for accomplishing this are other common features of good school performance.

REWARD GOOD PERFORMANCE

Al Klingenberg, superintendent in Lake Forest, is a very down-to-earth person who lives in a rather upscale suburban community. He has an unusual ability to convey a supportive attitude, yet his standards of performance and sense of expectations are equally obvious. The combination is powerful. Al meets with his school board to convince them to tax community residents for the highest teacher salaries in the area. His justification is that the district is delivering the highest performance. The proof is in test scores and surveys of parents and teachers. He also argues that the district's comfortable staff relations contribute to this good performance and that the board's confidence and the support of the staff are essential to those relationships. In return, the district is getting more than its money's worth.

This emphasis on good relationships and teamwork with recognition and reward for good performance is another common characteristic of successful districts. By actively using teamwork and support among board members, administrators, and teachers, Al Klingenberg avoids the controversy of collective bargaining and channels this energy into the educational program and performance. Student learning, parent satisfaction, teacher morale, and productivity pull the circle together, and give his board good reason for being willing to fund fair teacher salaries in exchange for the learning that is being achieved and the satisfaction of parents and teachers.

Lake Forest performance was already at a fairly high level when Al took over in 1971; gains have not been as dramatic as those in North Chicago and Hazel Crest. Nevertheless, improvements have been substantial in virtually every subject and grade, and in parent satisfaction, public confidence, teacher morale, and job satisfaction. When Al took office in 1971, he inherited a controversial school closing, a defeated referendum, the need for immediate budget cuts of 25 percent, and early retirement of the previous superintendent. Nevertheless, eighth grade equivalent scores rose from 10.9 to 12.9 from 1974–1975 to 1985–1986, compared with a national average of 8.8. Average annual growth rates currently are 13 to 14 months per year, compared with an average of 12 months in the late 1970s and early 1980s and a national average of 10 months. Several former high school courses have been moved down to the junior high school (e.g., foreign languages and advanced math).

Most remarkable in my own experience (I served on the board in this district for seven years) is the combination of an extremely participative and supportive management style with merit pay that recognizes and rewards good teachers in a system that is highly selective in recruiting, and demanding and supportive in teacher evaluation. The results are a high level of positive reinforcement internally and district accomplishments that continue to be recognized by national and local awards for excellence.

MORE EXAMPLES

Lombard is a middle-class suburb in a prosperous area of industry and research. Starting from an already successful pattern of 11 to 12 months of growth per year in the late 1970s and early 1980s, Lombard has increased student achievement to a growth rate of 13 to 15 months annually.

Zion, founded in the nineteenth century as a religious utopia, has changed from virtually all white to racially mixed and working class. Since 1973 it has doubled the rate of student learning, from 6 months to 12 months annually.

These and other districts implementing the governance-management-performance system have been assessed through an outside audit of student learning, using test data analysis and parent/teacher satisfaction surveys.

NATIONAL SCOPE

Although much of my experience with schools is in the Midwest, I have worked with public institutions as far away as Europe and Canada, and with teachers, administrators, and board members throughout this country. The patterns of changing requirements in school administration—for more teamwork and support, accountability and communication, and documented performance information—are clearly national trends. I have seen similar circumstances and results in schools and districts across the country. While the timing and intensity may be different, the impact of teacher unions, more assertive school boards, public concern, and reform legislation are nearly universal. My experience with a national sampling of board members, administrators, and teachers representing every state has convinced me of a common pattern of problems and solutions, even in districts as far apart as New York and California.

In Williamsburg, Virginia, the school board president described her frustration at being unable to get the superintendent to open up to the board and staff in exactly the words I had heard this problem described by the school board president in DuPage County, west of Chicago. The superintendent in Apache Junction, Arizona, turned around a district that had had 12 superintendents in 11 years by using the same strategy of measuring performance and building teamwork that I have seen work successfully across the country.

Recently an older principal asked me to keep a secret from her board; she was aware that some key performance indicators were not entirely favorable. The superintendent in this same district later explained to me that this principal would like to go back to the old era when the superintendent's job was to keep information secret from the board—a style he described as "running the district on a wing and a prayer." This was the style in industry a century ago: Don't tell the employees or the board anything; keep it secret, and use your authority to get a good job done.

Now we are entering a new era of participative and results-oriented school management—bringing a renaissance of public management to America's schools, finally applying the scientific method and behavioral sciences to measuring results and supporting improvement.

If the measurement and management system described in this book were applied in every American school, we would be achieving a full year's growth annually everywhere. These results could be replicated in schools and districts across the country, giving America the school performance we need to solve social problems and ensure continued economic progress. This would substantially raise the performance of many suburban and rural districts. It would turn around results in America's urban schools, many of which are achieving no more than half a year of growth for a year in school. This would be the most valuable contribution we could make to the children of our cities, and to our nation's most pressing social and economic problems, reducing the underclass in our big cities, giving America the trained workers we need for global competition, and containing the cost of domestic social services within limits we can afford. The public management revolution beginning in schools will give America the educated citizens we need for the future, and eventually lead to dramatic productivity improvements in all of America's public services that will be comparable with those of our farms and factories earlier.

II

The American Dream
Renewed

3

History: From Authority to Chaos to Management

Every school district in America is being affected by antiauthoritarian trends among teachers, students, and parents. These new circumstances are turning upside down the traditional power structure of America's school districts, which typically depended on the authority of a single individual in each district, the superintendent, and in each school, the principal, to whom everyone else was subordinate.

Even the school board often took orders from the superintendent. One principal told me that he was hired by an out-of-town district; when the superintendent told him to report for duty, he asked if it wouldn't be prudent to wait until the board approved his appointment. The superintendent answered, "Any board member who doesn't approve an appointment I make won't be on the board very long." This is only slightly exaggerated as an example of the authority superintendents typically enjoyed over their boards. Another story illustrating traditional superintendent authority is the "two lunch" system of dismissing staff members described to me by a teacher. The superintendent in that district was known to have lunch with a teacher if his or her performance was felt to be unsatisfactory. The restaurant setting made it more difficult for outbursts to occur. The first lunch was a warning, the second meant dismissal; everyone knew what was coming.

One board president told me that the superintendent—an Eisenhower-type leader of impeccable moral standing and integrity, but accustomed to having his authority accepted and endorsed by the board—simply disappeared once when the board disagreed with him. Searching the corridors of the school, they finally found him in the men's room. He told them if they ever disagreed with him again, he would leave permanently. This authority is not unlike that enjoyed by turn-of-the-century factory foremen, but you would have to go back almost a century to find it common. The change in schools occurred later, but more suddenly. And it has been just as difficult for school administrators as it was for businessmen to accept the need for participative management and performance measures.

One example of the change is that superintendents and principals now sometimes have to ask teachers when they can meet with them, because the workday is so circumscribed by negotiated contracts. Another example is the high turnover rate of superintendents, many fired by assertive school boards demanding more open communication, more information on what is going on in the district, and a more substantial role in decision making.

As I explained my management system to a group of administrators in a suburban district, a few years ago, two principals became visibly irritated. One said that he would never show the school board test scores: although he did not explain, I believe he felt this would be to question his own integrity and ability to manage the school, perhaps in much the same way that business owners of Henry Ford's era resisted public reporting of profits and sales. The other principal stood up in exasperation as I was talking about surveying parents and said, "My gosh, if you want to ask parents what they think, next you'll be wanting to ask teachers!" It was beyond his comprehension that those who had previously been expected to accept the authority of the principal without question should now be encouraged to express opinions that might include how well the principal was doing his or her job.

These examples are not meant to poke fun at school administrators or to make them seem old-fashioned; rather they are meant to indicate the magnitude of the change they face. Because unions were able to take over the existing membership of the National Education Association during the antiauthoritarian 1960s, teacher unions achieved almost total membership virtually overnight.

There are many different opinions about authority, an interesting discussion that I must gloss over in this description. There has been a long history of declining authority in organizations of all kinds; schools are the current target. Unfortunately, because this decline coincided with changes in our cities, we have experienced a national decline of school performance at a time when it is more important than it used to be, and in a way that has horribly impacted our big cities and their residents, threatening to leave America unable to compete in the world economy. These impacts have been extremely severe, America's worst moral failings of the twentieth century, something we must reverse as our highest national priority.

THE CAUSES OF DECLINE

When teacher unions pulled the rug out from under traditional school administration, many districts, especially in big cities, were thrown into a turmoil of essentially no management. Traditionally unfair and ineffective evaluation was stopped completely. At the same time, many cities were changing from their turn-of-the-century ethnic groups and receiving large numbers of blacks and Hispanics. Naturally this presented challenges to the schools and required different kinds of teaching talent and motivation. Schools failed to adapt. The combination has marred the lives of millions of students, contributing to the existence of an underdeveloped country in the heart of most American cities that is pulling down our national economy and threatening to create a permanent underclass. It has given a further handicap to those Americans already disadvantaged by a history of slavery and deprivation and to others whose education is more challenging because they are not yet literate in the English language. For the land of freedom and opportunity to tolerate this injustice is horrifying. The problem is made worse by the loss of jobs that were once available to those without much education (for instance, in the steel industry). A combination of declining school performance and loss of the jobs that might have given these people decent wages, has been devastating.

Governance policies, management techniques, and performance measures—developed, tested and proven in practice—are now achieving improvements in school productivity comparable with those which our country achieved earlier in this century in agriculture and industry. Some of these school districts are in big cities; yet their students are learning at above-average rates. This proves that the root of the problem is in the schools and how they are managed, not in the inability of students to learn. The achievements of urban communities demonstrate that their students can achieve academically at the same rate as their counterparts in the suburbs. There is nothing wrong with these students that good schools cannot overcome.

AMERICA'S CHANGING SCHOOL BOARDS

As a result of these changes, traditional authoritarian superintendents are being replaced by those willing to open up communication and provide information. The change is a fundamental reform of American democracy, as important to our future progress and success as the original revolution that brought democracy to America. While the timing and specific local events vary, there is a common pattern of transition from tradition to chaos to modern school governance.

Tradition

Traditional school boards typically delegated confidently to the superintendent. His authority covered whatever action was required to maintain good performance inside the organization. These were known as "rubber stamp" boards, and often were described as having a "cozy" relationship. University trustees have often followed a similar pattern: appointment is an honor and 100 percent delegation is expected in return. Erosion of the superintendent's authority through teacher unions and more assertive school boards, especially their women members, spurred on by public concern, make this kind of board a dying breed.

Chaos

In place of the traditional relationship, many districts have found themselves in a period of chaos. Sometimes this follows the first teachers' strike, school closing, fired superintendent or defeated referendum. Sometimes a period of board overinvolvement follows, with a quick succession of superintendents, long meetings, and controversy on a variety of subjects. While some districts have maintained reasonably good performance in spite of chaos at the top, others have failed. While the conflict in some districts is conspicuous and long-term, in others it is less obvious and shorter. Although some board members may be attracted to the conflict, this condition may cause an erosion in the quality of people willing to serve on school boards, since this kind of board service is very demanding and not very satisfying.

Modern

Replacing both tradition and chaos is a modern school board whose confidence in and support for district administrators is based on objective performance information and a competent, responsive internal management system. Analysis of test scores and periodic surveys of parents and teachers provide the board with the educational counterpart of a profit-and-loss statement for a business board of directors; an outside audit assures accuracy in these comparisons. This kind of board has time to deal with substantive educational issues. Careful analysis of test scores documents where learning is occurring and identifies potential improvement opportunities that become priorities for action. Surveys of parents and teachers provide qualitative information on customer and staff satisfaction. Together, these key indicators provide the basis for planning, along with such other data as attendance and dropout rates, and cost analyses. Communication, participation, teamwork, trust, and confidence characterize relationships in these districts, and substantial improvements are being achieved in learning. Board members are more satisfied and productive, less burdened with adversarial, time-consuming meetings and complaints from teachers and parents, and able to delegate with confidence to the district's management team and faculty.

THE SCHOOL MANAGEMENT TRANSITION

Schools are going through a transition much like that of business management half a century earlier—from an authoritarian approach to one involving more analytical techniques, better measures of results, and stricter accountability—yet with more concern for human relations and for people as employees and customers. The authoritarian style survived in schools until superintendents were jerked abruptly into the twentieth century by teacher unions in the 1960s. More assertive school boards—spurred by women members and publicity about declining test scores—also helped.

During the 1960s and 1970s superintendents lost their jobs with alarming frequency; average tenure declined to only a few years. Early retirements became common as older superintendents chose (or were chosen) not to face new management requirements. Paternalistic father figures are immortalized in oil paintings in administrative centers that bear their names. Look closely at the dates, and you will find their retirement often came soon after the first school closing, defeated referendum, or teacher's strike. The assertiveness of teacher unions in the 1960s and 1970s generated a similar assertiveness of school board members, many of them women, during the 1970s and 1980s. The demands of these board members came from the other side of the organization—asking superintendents to open up communication, to improve responsiveness to both community and staff, and to measure and improve performance, especially learning.

In the transition required of school management, superintendents and other administrators were caught on the battlefield. The national PTA, which had selected schools as its base of operations to help children, often found itself caught in the collective bargaining warfare. Superintendents were understandably confused. Their power historically came from defending teachers to the public, and in return asking teachers for support. Obviously that political equation no longer worked in an era of collective bargaining.

Superintendents and principals had enjoyed almost unlimited authority, much as factory managers did before the turn of the century. They simply took action on whatever they decided needed to be done. It is surprising that teachers tolerated this level of authority for decades after it virtually disappeared from much of industry. It seems to me completely appropriate for unions to have successfully terminated this era. But the problem is that nothing has taken the place of the traditional mechanisms for building support and assuring good performance in the absence of the traditional authority. Superintendents, confused when teachers turned on them in the first strike, could not formulate an appropriate response. Their natural instinct was to fight back.

School boards were often drawn into the controversy. "If those teachers want to fight, we'll show them what a real fight is," I heard one school board member say. "If teachers want to talk across the bargaining table, then that's the only place I'll speak to them," I heard from a superintendent. These natural reactions of school boards and superintendents made it difficult for them to perceive the new management requirements growing out of the new circumstances of education. Sometimes they became more secretive and closed, rather than more open and communicative. This seemed the worst time to analyze and use performance information, since they felt under attack and threatened by loss of authority.

The new model replaces traditional authoritarian school administration. Autocratic superintendents and principals, with almost unlimited power and authority, served American education well in an earlier era, and probably cost less than the management system described in this book. But it is unlikely that teachers will ever again accept that kind of authority. There is no point in trying to go back.

4

Background: My Personal Odyssey to Public Management

Much has been written about the crisis in American education, but less about the solution. Of course, the answer is not to dwell on the problems, but to find solutions that have worked successfully, and to find out why they are successful.

Still on the subject of history, but on a more personal note, I would like to share with you the odyssey that led me to public management. My experience with a major consulting firm, first in industry and later in education and government, led me to understand that America's schools and public services need to be managed. Since 1973 I have worked with thousands of educators to develop, test, and prove a measurement and management system for schools. I have had the opportunity to apply the system as a school board member and parent in the district where my four children attend school—and in hundreds of other urban, rural, and suburban schools and districts across the country.

When my four children started school in the early 1970s, fundamental changes were forcing America's schools, rather suddenly, into the twentieth century of participative, results-oriented management. From my management background I could see that simple, proven management techniques, such as measuring results, developing people, and asking customers and staff what they want, were unknown in schools and other public services. They simply had not developed and applied the kind of management techniques that made American industry the world leader.

Coming into the management of public services from a background of corporate planning and organization for business, I could see opportunities—in virtually unmanaged public services—for the application of simple, proven management techniques. Simply put, the same revolution that overtook agriculture and industry during the past century could be applied to public services—the scientific method to measure results and the psychology of human development to improve performance.

MANAGEMENT IN EUROPE AND AMERICA

My own perception of the need for public management grew out of early career experiences. As an economics major at Cornell University I learned to be skeptical of the motives and consequences of capitalism. Yet a few years later—when I had the opportunity to live and work for a summer in Zurich, Switzerland—it was obvious that, from the perspective of Europe, America's strength lay in its business management capability. From that perspective, conscious that we had saved Europe in two world wars, America looked remarkably prosperous and successful in areas that everyone desires: food, housing, automobiles, and so on.

Equally obvious, Europe's public services were better than ours. Most conspicuous was city planning: developmental control and use of urban spaces are generally far better in European cities than in their counterparts in the United States. It was apparent in Switzerland that care for the environment, and concern for social well-being, even in a very commercially oriented country, were much greater than in the United States. So I concluded that America's need, measured on a world scale, was more for stronger public services and less for criticizing business.

The second event that pushed me in the direction of strengthening public service performance and management was working as Jim Allen's assistant. As one of the founders of Booz, Allen & Hamilton, he had inherited from Ed Booz and Walter Dill Scott[1] (president of Northwestern University) an emphasis on people as the driving force of organization and management. This humanistic approach emphasized the development of employees and a satisfying, productive, motivating workplace, as well as people as customers with an emphasis on satisfying their needs and desires, perhaps best expressed in the old department store adages "Give the customer what she wants" and "The customer is always right."

Jim Allen asked me to help plan the transition of Northwestern's School of Business, under the leadership of newly appointed Dean John Barr, to a School of Management that would embrace the need for public management as well as business training. The school's Advisory Council (mostly chief executives from leading companies, and a few public servants) agreed with the concept that public services needed to be managed just as much as business. America's management education resources were out of balance, aimed almost entirely at business and only to a modest and inadequate extent at public services.

Northwestern went on to adopt this concept as part of its strategy for working up to the first rank of America's graduate business schools. Other schools emulated the concept, many now calling themselves schools of management rather than schools of business. Stanford has also been particularly successful. Other universities have created separate public management training institutions, such as Harvard's Kennedy School of Public Policy, in an effort to address the problem. I do not know which solution will ultimately produce better results; probably there is a place for both. We need these experiments and others to achieve a better balance between America's business and public management education resources. There is still much to be done.

During the 1960s and 1970s I had the opportunity to apply my concept of public management in education and government in this country and in Europe. Working with American universities was particularly exciting during the 1960s, when student activists were turning universities upside down with their demands for participatory democracy and anger over the Vietnam War. Then I moved to England, to head Booz Allen's general management consulting there, and had an opportunity to reorganize two local governments: the boroughs of Islington (in London) and Stockport (in Manchester). This opened my eyes to the needs for planning and analysis of performance and for strengthening personnel evaluation, development, and compensation in government.

We were able to initiate new concepts that have since become standard practice in English local government: general management, corporate planning, mission and purpose, goals and objectives, analyzing improvement opportunities, performance information, a personnel function, staff development, evaluation and performance-based compensation; and strong leadership positions in housing, city planning, social services, and the mechanics of keeping cities running, such as highways, sewers, refuse, and water. These four groups of local government services have markedly different management requirements, and therefore benefit from being grouped separately under leadership appropriate to their nature. For example, city planning requires an unusually long-range and broad-based social and economic perspective, whereas street cleaning and highway repair are more mechanical and measurable, with large labor forces that need to be controlled carefully to be sure the public is getting its money's worth. Social services benefited most of all from being consolidated and decentralized to neighborhood units of about 10,000–15,000 people to be more cost-effective.

Since 1973 I have had the opportunity to adapt, test, and prove my concept of public management in America's schools—with the help of thousands of teachers, administrators, board members, parents, and students in hundreds of schools and districts across the country. Helped by Northwestern University and the Illinois and national associations of school boards and administrators, I have had the opportunity to write several books, to develop and teach school and public management courses, and to serve as a school board member. As a result I have been able to develop, refine, and communicate a system of school governance, management, and performance and the policies, plans, and measures to implement it successfully in practice—the experience this book reports.

My management consulting experience taught me to look at people as customers and staff, at their needs, desires, attitudes, and concerns, as the starting point for analyzing an organization. My background in economics supported analyzing performance using the best available indicators, quantitative if possible. So naturally, when I began working with the schools, I started by talking to those on the ground floor of the organization—students, parents, teachers, and administrators—to find out their perceptions and concerns. This is the foundation for the ideas in this book and the recommended management system.

I have been aided in understanding the teacher's point of view by Dolores Solovy, founder and head of the Kohl Teacher Center, and by my colleagues in Phi Delta Kappa, the national fraternity of professional educators, at Northwestern University and throughout the Chicago area, especially Jean Damisch, Pat Hastings, Nina Koelpin, Joe Boyd, and David Whiting. In addition to the courses I have taught in school and public management at Northwestern University, these individuals have helped me to understand the perspective of teachers, their dedication to improvement and development, and their inherently conscientious responsibility for performance. This coexists with the seemingly opposite position of unions defending teachers against authority, sometimes by eliminating all evaluation procedures. These are not contradictory positions if one assumes that the evaluation procedures being objected to are in fact unfair, as many were, and that excessive administrative authority was sometimes abused.

A few leading superintendents and board members have been able to drive forward the public management revolution beginning in schools. But their districts are only a tiny proportion of the total. To realize the full national benefits of improved school performance, we must reach a far larger audience. To do so requires communicating this message to a large number of people: citizens and educators, those receiving the service and those responsible for delivering it.

This book is designed to broaden our reach in communicating this message of the vital implications for America's future, and in refining the presentation of policies, techniques, and measures to make them more readily understandable to more people. I hope to reach those directly responsible—school board members and administrators—and the larger audience needed if the message is going to get to those who can really apply it across the country, eventually to every school in America.

RESPONSIVENESS TO CUSTOMERS—SUPPORT FOR STAFF

One of the impressions I have gained as a result of crossing back and forth between business and public service since 1964 is that management in successful organizations of all kinds emphasizes responsibility to customers and support of staff. In the late 1960s, when I first began to reorganize management for British local government, I looked for the kinds of customer-oriented performance data I had been accustomed to finding in American businesses. How large was the market? What were the trends? What did the customer need? What were the economics of delivering the product or service? None of this was available. It seemed a natural opportunity to create a corporate planning function devoted to assembling this information, so that planning could be based on solid data. In effect, a local government needed to define what business it was in, based on the needs of the people it was serving, then to figure out how close it was to meeting those needs, and act to meet the difference.

For example, in the London borough of Islington, statistics indicated that 37 percent of the housing was in unsatisfactory condition. There were more than 20,000 people on the waiting list for public housing, in a population of about 200,000. These simple statistics were the driving force behind a massive housing program that has since reduced unsatisfactory housing to less than 17 percent.

Successful businesses devote a substantial amount of time and attention to selecting, motivating, developing, and supporting their staff, so that each individual's success can lead to the success of the organization as a whole. I often think about this when I read about the difficulties teachers have. I have had many interviews with teachers in which they complain about shortages of supplies and about materials they have to buy themselves. It sometimes seems that administrators, especially in big cities, are working against the teachers or are impeding their success, rather than seeing themselves, as they should, as a support system for teaching effectiveness. I still find it helpful to think of the simple concept of management as the linkage between customers and staff, assuring responsiveness to the one and support for the other. You can see obvious implications of this concept for other public services, such as the criminal justice system and social services. Prisons seem to create more problems than they solve, and American welfare programs may have done more to create an underclass than to solve the problem.

While I was working with Jim Allen in 1966 to plan the School of Management for Northwestern University, as we were discussing the meaning of management, he said, "Isn't it really all people?" Obviously this reflects the humanistic orientation of the Renaissance and the lessons Jim had probably learned from Walter Dill Scott, one of the pioneers in applying the scientific method to human behavior. I could not help but agree, and yet I argued that results are also important, because they give meaning to a person's involvement in an organization. Accomplishments, progress, performance—these are the American version of fundamental values, instead of the family position, land-ownership, and inherited titles of Europe. This concept of the American Dream is still alive and well, and relevant to our needs for public management today.

NOTE

1. Ed Booz was Scott's assistant in developing the original Army Alpha and Beta tests, an example of America's emphasis on talent and merit instead of family and social rank, credited with being one of the factors behind America's success in World War I. Scott helped to create personnel and marketing management and served as president of Northwestern University during the 1920s and 1930s.

5

Renaissance: Democratic, Pragmatic, and Progressive

Modern history since the Renaissance could be characterized as a trend of declining authority and growing freedom. Medieval concepts of church and state and moral limits on freedom of choice seem impossibly restrictive in a modern world of existentialist values, civil rights, womens' liberation, virtually everything open to choice and negotiation. Americans' search for personal success through self-help is giving way to more concern with community and environment, and well it should. Our history is full of social responsibility added to personal ambition, though the former is usually preceded by the latter, often with a generation or two separating social contribution from personal success.

The declining authority of school administrators should be seen as one more step in the inevitable course of history away from authority and toward freedom. It should be celebrated along with America's other successes in civil rights, the feminist movement, and the widening freedom of choice generally available in a modern society.

We must also recognize the broader educational opportunities of children today, largely because of television, in spite of how we fear and criticize this still new and somewhat frightening medium. How else can you explain the unwillingness of American and Soviet citizens to fight in unjustified wars in Vietnam and Afghanistan? Children are benefiting from the availability of television in spite of our criticism of the medium. A University of Chicago math project has found that a majority of inner-city children can count to 100 by the time they reach school. The curriculum proposes to teach them to count to 15. Perhaps this is one of the reasons they are dropping out as soon as they can.

At the end of this chapter is a historical note on the relevance of some turn-of-the-century American leaders—Walter Dill Scott, William James, and John Dewey—to our current problems of school reform and public management. America's democratic, progressive, and pragmatic traditions are still needed, and are reflected in the public management platform presented this chapter.

The American tradition of national democracy, still respected and increasingly emulated around the world, must be extended to our local communities. The two-tier model of local government initiated in England more than a century ago must be adapted and applied in America. Public services and local schools, especially social services, must be decentralized to communities and neighborhoods. The unfinished turn-of-the-century reform that helped to stimulate the industrial and agricultural revolutions and carried them forward to positive conclusions must be extended to America's schools and cities. The Progressive tradition of making things better must be carried forward to make the current residents of our cities, mostly African-American and Hispanic, as successful as America's earlier immigrants. We need to continue the pragmatic tradition of dealing with a situation as it is and seeking positive results, whatever the circumstances. America's cities and schools can be effective and well managed, and our international economic competitiveness and domestic social progress can be continued.

Public management is a political philosophy to replace authority, bureaucracy, conflict, and decline with teamwork and success. It uses the best of America's traditions—democratic, pragmatic, and Progressive—implemented through governance policies, participative management, and performance measures.

SOCIAL, ECONOMIC, AND POLITICAL TRENDS TOWARD PUBLIC MANAGEMENT

Three broad areas of trends—social, economic, and political—are causing the public management revolution to come of age in America:

- Rising concern with community and environment
- Growing recognition of a postindustrial global economy of information and services
- Renewed interest in Progressive reform of schools and public services.

Social trends in America are toward responsibility and concern for community and the environment. Antiauthoritarian, prosocial justice feelings of the 1960s are returning as baby boomers come into positions of power. Neighborhood organizations grow in strength and number, and America's companies are beginning to take consumer interests in environmental protection and safe products more seriously.

Economic trends also favor public services, as we increasingly recognize that they represent the largest part of our economy. We still do not have enough health care, education, and other public services, whereas we have learned how to feed ourselves and provide enough products (some think too much and too many). The American economy is already comprised mainly of information and services, most of them public. In a postindustrial society and global economy most of us now work in services, with industry rapidly following agriculture as a declining and relatively small part of the total economy. These are not signs of decline but simply inevitable trends, as automation replaces workers in factories as it did labor on farms. Now we must use these people in productive public service and educational jobs, if economic progress is to continue.

Think of history as an hourglass in which the first shift of sand flowing from top to bottom was away from the authoritarian class structure of Europe and into the freedom and equality of participative democracy in America. Then the hourglass turned over, and the flow was from agriculture to industry, as people moved from farms with their improving productivity into factories to meet the material needs of the people. The smart countries understood this, and moved quickly in this direction; others lag behind, and some still have not made the change. Now the hourglass has turned again, this time flowing from industry into public services and schools. American employment today is 3 percent on farms, 25 percent in industry, and 72 percent in managerial, professional, and service occupations.

Political trends are increasingly demanding accountability and performance of public services. Public services are the focal point of attention now that industry is following agriculture as a declining proportion of our economy. Political attitudes in America increasingly are antibureaucratic and antiauthoritarian. These factors argue for a return of the Progressive reform era as the Cold War winds down and the class struggle is seen to be over. Exploitation of the worker is no longer socially profitable. Success is dependent on development of everyone. The renaissance of public management will see emphasis on humanism and the scientific method, like the participative and results-oriented management that led to America's productivity improvements in agriculture and industry. We will find ways to put American public services on the line for good performance and to recognize and reward that performance when it is demonstrated. We do not just want services; we want services that are well managed and effective. Successful merit pay plans in school districts are already doing this, but they are few in number. Once Americans realize the payoff from improved public service performance, we will be less skittish about adequate salaries to attract the talent that is needed to get the job done. This is a lesson

Russia learned on collective farms: without an incentive, farmers do not produce much.

These trends are being aided by continuation of the antiauthoritarianism that has spanned centuries in Western history. The decline of authority that began with Joan of Arc is continuing and accelerating in civil rights, women's rights, and other movements. This is opening new expectations—for example, in the achievements of America's handicapped children, now out of closets and in school, making remarkable progress never before thought possible. Overall school performance can also be improved dramatically.

AGRICULTURE, INDUSTRY, AND PUBLIC SERVICES

Business schools have their roots in the Progressive era of America's efforts to reform agriculture, industry, and public services shortly after the turn of the century. We succeeded in agriculture and industry. But public services were the victim of distractions: World War I, the Roaring Twenties, the Depression, World War II, and the Cold War. Perhaps now, with thawing of the Cold War, we will be able to return to this third priority.

Obviously changes are needed in agriculture and industry as well. But America's public services have never achieved the productivity improvements that have been accomplished in factories and on farms. From my experience, we could. In some respects public services will be a more demanding management challenge than those in agriculture and industry. Services are characteristically more difficult to define and measure. Public services often deal with problems that have not been solved by private initiative. They are generally people-intensive and therefore often difficult to manage. Many of their purposes and results—no matter how well defined—are still difficult to evaluate—and to achieve. Under these circumstances, good management has an even greater payoff. It is not possible to fall back on economics, patents, or distinctive marketing strategies. Management in public services is a more singular determinant of success and improved productivity than it is in business, where a good product, patent protection, technology, or a market niche can offset poor management.

It is ironic but important for Americans to recognize that we have worked ourselves out of employment in areas that we know how to manage well and into fields that are not very well managed—out of agriculture and industry and into public services. We must translate management know-how to meet the needs of public services.

APPLYING THE MODEL TO OTHER PUBLIC SERVICES

The three-part system of board policies, management techniques, and performance measures can be the basis for improvement in other public services. Responsiveness to the customer, measured by surveys; productivity and key performance indicators such as learning; a concept of mission and purpose, teamwork and accountability, established by board policy and chief executive leadership: these management techniques are widely applicable. Measurement of results—as a way of forcing definition of mission and purpose and providing feedback on accomplishments—must be added to the traditional American distinction between policy and administration.

As in agriculture and industry, measures of performance would do more to increase productivity than perhaps any other single factor, especially if combined with a more participative and humane style of management like that which has evolved in successful companies over the past several decades.

A NATIONAL STRATEGY FOR TEAMWORK AND SUCCESS

The public management revolution beginning in America's schools is strengthening local democracy and improving school performance. This is providing a new agenda for America's domestic progress and success, especially timely now that the Cold War seems to be winding down. Beginning in schools, dramatic public service performance improvements are being achieved. The end of the class struggle and the Cold War opens the door to a new era for America. As the agricultural revolution ended the era of peasants, so the industrial revolution has finally ended the era of workers. In the postindustrial world, most of us will be professionals in a global economy of information and services; very few will work on farms or in factories. When the Communist bloc wants to join us instead of fight us, it means the principal dialectic of the twentieth century is over. And when business executives speak out in favor of education, it is not to exploit the workers but because they realize we all benefit from a better-educated society.

America is entering its third phase of development. A strategy of teamwork and success is needed. Instead of fighting between labor and capital or against communism, we must work together for mutual progress. The engine of upward mobility and continued progress in America will be education, but not in its traditional authoritarian form. Individualism and participative democracy will break out in schools, catching them up with what happened at the managerial and professional level of companies decades ago. The behavioral sciences will be discovered. Participative and results-oriented management has already been developed and successfully applied, and will become virtually universal. School performance will rise dramatically.

The model of governance, management, and performance described in this book—with the policies, plans, and measures to implement it successfully—will be applied to all public services. This will have as great an impact on their productivity as the agricultural and industrial revolutions did on the productivity of farms and factories. Standards of living and quality of life will rise dramatically because of the improved productivity of public services. America's urban crisis, underclass, and civil rights problems will be solved.

Good schools and the public management revolution can solve the urban crisis, establish America's economic competitiveness, restart civil rights progress—and provide a solid foundation for our continued economic success and social progress. In a democracy, expectations determine the quality of public services. At stake are the progress and success of America.

YOU ARE NEEDED

This book speaks to every American concerned about our public schools. In a democracy, we are still ultimately responsible for the quality of public services, through the expectations and standards we apply to their performance and management. Good school performance even in urban areas is possible, and it is essential to America's continued social progress and economic success.

You are the most important factor to achieving this progress. Every American citizen, whether parent and taxpayer, teacher, administrator, or board member, must raise his or her standards and expectations for school performance and management. You do not have to tune your own carburetor to know whether your car's milage is satisfactory. Similarly, you do not have to manage the school or teach a class. Just expect, and if necessary demand, that your school and district live up to the performance and management standards detailed in this book.

HISTORICAL NOTE

Walter Dill Scott was president of Northwestern University from 1920 to 1940. The world's first professor of applied psychology, he developed the Army Alpha and Beta tests, which organized the United States Army in World War I on the basis of merit, demonstrating the superiority of this to Europe's tradition of basing military rank on family background and status. His books on marketing and personnel helped to create these functions in business. As a teacher with interests in psychology, philosophy, and progress, you might consider him a counterpart of John Dewey at Chicago and of William James at Harvard. Dill is credited with inventing management consulting through his own firm and as mentor to Jim Allen and Ed Booz. He symbolizes a commitment to teamwork and success with a humanistic and pragmatic approach emphasizing results.

William James was the turn-of-the-century Harvard philosopher and psychologist whose pragmatic philosophy provided the foundation of situation- and results-oriented analysis on which the case study method of the Harvard Business School is based.

John Dewey at the University of Chicago (and Michigan and Columbia) also began in psychology, added to the pragmatic philosophy of William James, and applied the behavioral science to schools.

The ideas of these three men have a surprising current relevance (along with the Progressive era of Teddy Roosevelt and Woodrow Wilson) as America's schools enter a period of replacing authority with freedom of choice and empowerment of teachers with the accompanying need for analyzing situations, setting objectives, and measuring results. The Renaissance breadth of interest and humanism of these turn-of-the-century American leaders and our democratic, pragmatic, and Progressive traditions are worth reconsidering as we seek ways to reform schools, cities, and other public services, to assure America's continued progress and success with economic competitiveness and equal opportunity.

III

Introduction to the Public Management Revolution Beginning in America's Schools

6

What: Applying Participative, Results-Oriented Management

A public management revolution that has profound implications for our future economic success and social progress is beginning in America's schools. Our schools are being turned upside down by teachers who no longer accept traditional authoritarian school administration and by board members unwilling to serve merely as "rubber stamps" for the superintendent's authority. The combination has caused conflict and decline in the past few decades. Out of this chaos is emerging a system of school governance, management, and performance with the democratic board policies, participative management practices, and pragmatic performance measures needed to implement it successfully.

The public management revolution extends the original American Revolution of freedom and democracy to local public services and schools. Instead of government being the authority telling us what to do, public services are seen as exactly that—services to the public—with citizens as customers and taxpayers. This concept turns public services upside down. Their purpose is to serve rather than to control the public. This is something that America showed the world with our national democratic experiment two centuries ago. But it has not always flowed down to the local level of schools and public services. Now is the time.

In this concept of public management, it is up to citizens, both customers and staff, to judge the performance of the services being provided. The people, not bureaucrats and authorities, are in charge. Purposes are expressed and measured in results: responsiveness to the needs and desires of customers, satisfaction and productivity of staff, and cost-effectiveness for taxpayers. In schools, the public management concept is realized through a strategy of teamwork and success implemented through democratic governance, participative management, and measuring progress. The same concept can be applied to other public services—cities, states, federal government, justice, health care, and higher education.

The positive lessons of America's national democracy are only now reaching other countries of the world. But we have not yet extended the implications fully in our own country. There are important lessons for public services to learn from the agricultural and industrial revolutions, and the behavioral sciences and scientific method that fueled these trends. The public management revolution extends the following to schools and public services:

- The agricultural revolution of scientific measures to evaluate and improve productivity
- The industrial revolution of participative management to motivate and reward good performance
- The lessons already learned in these fields from application of the behavioral sciences and scientific method, both to define and measure results and to motivate and support improvement.

The reform of America's public services and schools is as important to our future success as the earlier stages of national democracy, industry, and agriculture were to our past.

The public management revolution has its immediate roots in the antiauthoritarian 1960s, when teacher unions overthrew the authority of school administrators. And it draws on the best of America's history of national progress, pragmatic measures, and political freedom:

- Political freedom embodied in the constitution drafted by America's founding fathers
- Pragmatic philosophy exemplified by the psychologists William James, John Dewey, and Walter Dill Scott
- The concept of national progress that swept America during the administrations of Teddy Roosevelt and Woodrow Wilson.

Now, finally, there is something to take the place of traditional authoritarian school administration, the conflict and fragmentation of recent decades (e.g., teacher strikes), and mere political rhetoric and media show—a three-part system of participation, progress, and democracy:

- *Participative management* for teachers and administrators—positive support; fair evaluation, recognition, and reward; communication; teamwork; trust and confidence

• *Performance measures* for board and public—proof that a good job is being done, identifying improvement opportunities, justifying salaries and budgets
• *Democratic governance policies* and leadership—to foster teamwork, accountability, and success through participative management and performance measures.

This system gives teachers the freedom with responsibility promised by the American Revolution. It applies to schools pragmatic measures like those which improved the productivity of farms and factories in the agricultural and industrial revolutions. It brings to public services the techniques of participative management that have made American business and agriculture more productive and competitive. It applies the scientific method and behavioral sciences to schools and other public services.

America is increasingly recognizing the importance of education and other public services, not as ancillary functions in society but as the main sources of employment in a postindustrial society, and as the most critical functions for continued improvements in our quality of life, economic success, and social progress. This provides a new agenda for America's domestic progress and success, especially timely now that the Cold War is coming to an end. Beginning in schools, dramatic public service performance improvements are being achieved.

PARTICIPATION AND ACCOUNTABILITY

The solution to urban crisis and school failure, and to America's future progress and success, is a balance of participative management with performance measures and board accountability. The balance is between accountable schools for citizens and participative management for staff. On one hand, schools must perform effectively with demonstrably good results to justify the funding needed for good schools and fair salaries. On the other hand, teachers need supportive, participative management with planning, information, evaluation and compensation, recognition and reward, teamwork, trust and confidence, communication, and participation. The system is implemented through action on three levels—board, administrators, and teachers—to improve learning, confidence, morale, and cost-effectiveness—with students, parents, and teachers satisfied and taxpayers getting their money's worth.

This new concept of school governance, management, and performance is simplified in the triangle in Figure 1.

Inside these three components are the following:

1. *Accountable boards:* policies and leadership for teamwork and success, with boards evaluating performance (not just "rubber stamps")

Figure 1
The System

2. *Participative management:* positive support for teachers and administrators; performance-based planning, organization information, evaluation, and compensation

3. *Performance measures:* measures of learning, confidence, morale, and cost-effectiveness; plus an outside audit for credibility and as the catalyst for measurement and improvement.

The system is implemented through three levels of action:

Governance: The board's primary function is providing community representation and policy guidance, emphasizing people and results, to support superintendent leadership for accountability and teamwork.

Management: Communication, organization, planning, information, evaluation, and compensation provide positive support for administrators and teachers.

Performance: Progress is measured using multiple indicators for parent/teacher/student satisfaction, for student learning, and for costs. Information is used to build confidence, provide positive reinforcement, identify improvement opportunities, and justify expenditures.

These three levels of action can make every district, school, and student successful.

Participative management is used to encourage and support good performance with aggressive staff development, recruitment, and selection; positive recognition and reward; and performance-based organization, evaluation, and compensation. Performance measures build the confidence needed to delegate responsibility to the staff and to justify the funding needed for good schools and fair salaries—by showing where a good job is being done, identifying improvement opportunities, building confidence and morale, and actually improving performance. Fundamental benefits of history's most important lessons—behavioral sciences and the scientific method, for example—are applied to the way in which schools are governed, managed, and measured. The renaissance of scientific method and humanistic values is brought to local community schools and other public services. This system of board policies, management, plans and performance measures has three specific action steps.

1. *Replace traditional "rubber stamp" school boards, and the conflict of recent years, with teamwork and accountability.* Board policies for teamwork and accountability replace traditional "rubber stamp" school boards who took orders from all-powerful superintendents, and the conflict and fragmentation of recent years, to improve performance and relationships.

2. *Build a participative and results-oriented management system, to replace traditional authoritarian school administration.* A management system connects board and staff—with positive support for teachers and administrators—and a fair, effective system of planning, information, evaluation, and compensation—to implement policies of teamwork and accountability.

3. *Measure school results, starting at the bottom with parent/teacher satisfaction and student learning.* A third level of measuring performance is added to the traditional American distinction between policy and administration in public affairs. The formula of

$$\frac{\text{Learning} \times \text{Confidence} \times \text{Morale}}{\text{Cost}}$$

uses practical, proven measures for satisfaction and learning by surveying parents and teachers and analyzing test scores.

The planning process starts with a realistic assessment of performance and the situation in each school or department. Information provides a solid foundation for confidence and for identifying improvement opportunities. It justifies board confidence and the delegation of authority needed for participative management to be effective. Board and public support and appreciation are based on objective performance data. Positive support for teacher improvement and aggressive staff selection, recruitment, and development are also important features of the system. In effect, the board is offering fairness and support in exchange for measures of results and performance-based compensation. Consequently, there is greater overall productivity and increased job satisfaction for staff; an upward spiral of teamwork and success instead of conflict and decline.

This humane and participative, supportive, and responsive concept of school management puts a balanced emphasis on both people and results:

- Teamwork, communication, participation, trust, and confidence; supportive staff relationships; and responsiveness to constituents
- Accountability, evaluation, information, and responsibility for performance, documented with evidence; improvement opportunities identified and acted upon.

By using this system, thousands of teachers, administrators, and board members are currently achieving more effective schools, communication, and participation; positive management; accountable boards; motivated staff; satisfied parents; a confident public—and more student learning.

BACKGROUND

The system is based on 15 years of research and practical experience with schools and districts across the country in which board members, administrators, and teachers have successfully improved school performance through better management. The system has been documented in 2 books and 15 handbooks now used in every state and 20 foreign countries. I have used this background as well as my personal experience as a school board member; management consultant to business, government, and education in this country and in Europe; and a Harvard MBA to develop this system. It is not theoretical or experimental but fully implemented and proven, ready to be applied in every American school and public service. That application should involve every American citizen.

Of course this system of governance, management, and performance is only part of what it takes to make a quality school. But it is often the missing part, underdeveloped because American schools were administered in a traditional authoritarian style that was ended abruptly by teacher unions in the 1960s and has not been replaced. Like the universal joint in your car, it is a small but critically important ingredient. Substituting modern, participative, results-oriented management for traditional authoritarian administration has not yet happened in every school. It is the single most cost-effective thing we could do to turn around the declining performance of American schools, and to substantially improve their productivity. It does not mean there are not other things we should also do, just that this is the easiest and most productive. All we have to do is to apply techniques well known in other fields.

TRENDS AND CAUSES

This system of participative management with performance measures and board accountability has grown out of changes in the circumstances of American education that have created new management requirements:

- Protection for teachers won by unions
- More assertive and responsible school boards
- National concern about school performance, accountability, and reform
- Growing recognition of the importance of education for America's future.

Specific recommendations and implementation of the system vary from district to district. Nevertheless, there is a common framework of research, to help provide guidance and direction:

- Moving from traditional authoritarian school administration to participative and results-oriented management
- Replacing the conflict of recent years with teamwork among school boards, administrators, and teachers
- Adding a third component—measuring results—to board policy and the management process.

Changing management requirements for schools are being brought about by four main trends of American education in recent decades.

Teacher Protection Won by Unions

With the advent of teacher unions in the 1960s, the first reaction of many superintendents was to close their door to communication except through the bargaining process. Boards and superintendents were often lured into tough bargaining that strengthened the union and resulted in widespread and conspicuous conflict that was very difficult for the public to understand. Following a period of rapid turnover in superintendents and many early retirements, school administrators are now adjusting more positively to the necessary transition. Communication, teamwork, trust and confidence, fair and effective evaluation, and participative management are the right response to these new circumstances, rather than tough bargaining and adversarial, combative relationships among board, administration, and faculty.

More Assertive and Responsible School Boards

Partly in response to teacher unions, school boards are no longer willing to be subservient to the superintendent's authority. Instead, they are insisting on more open communication, responsiveness to needs and desires of parents and teachers, and board participation in decision making. Pressures on school administration from one side of the organization are being matched by those from the other.

National Concern about School Performance, Accountability and Reform

Beginning with the taxpayer revolt of the 1970s and accelerating through the 1980s, America's concern about school performance, whether taxpayers are getting their money's worth, and how school boards, administrators, and teachers can be held accountable contrasts with higher levels of satisfaction and test scores, and complacency or even apathy, in the 1950s.

Growing Recognition of the Importance of Education for the Future

This is the most recent and the most positive of the four trends, reflecting a fundamental perception of education as the driving force of a postindustrial society and a global economy of information and services. The rising stature of teachers is driving up salaries and finally causing action to correct the deficiencies of education in our big cities. Many American institutions have confronted and surmounted dramatic changes in the past few decades. Older industries marked by successful histories and authoritarian methods, such as automobiles and steel, have experienced similar transitions for different reasons. More important than the short-term dislocations that may be caused by these trends are the fundamentally changed management requirements of schools as a result, because these are the requirements we must meet in the future.

SCHOOL MANAGEMENT REQUIREMENTS

There are three new management requirements of schools today. Measuring performance is the most important. Second is a more humane and participative style of management. Third is accountable school boards that enforce performance measures and encourage participative management through their policies and behavior. These three requirements contrast with the history of school administration; thus the difficulty of change. Superintendents historically were expected to keep secret any information that might bear upon the performance of the district, such as test scores, or to present it in ways that no average citizen could understand.

The authoritarian style of leadership in which power was centered in a single individual, the superintendent or principal, with little written documentation of policies and procedures, survived in schools for decades after its demise in industry. School boards remained subservient to the superintendent. Now all this has changed. A new concept of performance, management, and governance is needed. From research, as well as personal experience as a school board member and management consultant to business, government, and education, I have reached three key conclusions about school management requirements:

1. *School performance needs to be measured* in order to provide a foundation for teamwork and accountability, adding a third level—measuring results—to the traditional American dichotomy between policy and administration. The focus should be on student learning and parent/teacher satisfaction, using a simple, practical, local measurement system that demonstrates accountability, documents results, improves performance, and justifies the funding needed for good schools and fair salaries.

2. *A positive management system is needed* to support teachers and administrators with planning, information, evaluation, and compensation, including more aggressive development and recruitment to ensure the talent needed to get the job done. Participation and support of staff are needed, rather than conflict and fragmentation, with recognition and reward for good performance. The system has two key parts:

• Communication, participation, responsiveness, teamwork, trust, and confidence

• Performance-based compensation, evaluation, and organization using objective information wherever possible.

3. *Board policy should stress teamwork and accountability*—productive relationships among board, superintendent, administrators, and teachers; leadership to prove that a good job is being done, improve performance, build confidence and morale—with boards evaluating superintendents on these criteria and not automatically supporting administrative authority. Critical to success is the board's understanding that its behavior must emphasize positive reinforcement and teamwork for the staff at the same time it demands performance measures proving that a good job is being done and, wherever possible, identifying improvement opportunities. In short, we need pragmatic measures for schools like those which led to America's success in agriculture and industry, with participative management and accountable boards—replacing traditional authoritarian school administration with a more participative and results-oriented approach.

RESULTS

The most remarkable thing about this system is not that it meets the new requirements of school governance, management, and performance. It also achieves dramatic performance improvements similar to those America showed the world in agriculture and industry. For example, 10 districts using the new system and monitoring performance over a period of 10 to 15 years have achieved, on average, 37 percent more learning. Growth rates have improved from an average of less than a year for a year in school to 13 or 14 months of growth per year, compared with a national average of 10 months. Three urban districts have succeeded in doubling the rate of student learning from approximately 6 months per year to 12 months per year. These results, duplicated in America's big cities, would go a long way toward solving our problems of the underclass, welfare, unemployment, and criminal justice. Certainly this is a better alternative than federal troops or deficits. The implications for urban property values would be dramatic if America's big cities had good schools.

These learning gains are matched by districts in suburban and rural areas. A rural district is getting achievement scores in the 80s even though the children have ability scores in the 50s. A suburban district has added two years of growth to eight years of education. Public confidence and parent satisfaction have shown substantial improvements. Teacher morale and job satisfaction show rising trends. These improvements in output have been achieved without more input. Cost-effectiveness has risen dramatically. It is possible to achieve much more productivity from our present expenditures on education. This is something our schools ought to be asked to demonstrate before we invest more money in them, even though that investment is well worth making once their productivity is demonstrated.

The performance improvements being realized with this governance-management-performance system are inspiring. The system meets the needs of both citizens and educators. For the public—citizens, parents, and taxpayers—there is a solid basis of accountability proving that a good job is being done with objective information. For educators—teachers and administrators—positive support, recognition, and reward make for satisfying professional productivity. Between these two sides of the equation, school board policies and superintendent leadership foster both teamwork and accountability with participative management and performance measures.

Wider application would result in a dramatic improvement of school productivity across the country, raising property values in America's cities and reducing costs of welfare, unemployment, and crime, helping to end the underclass and urban crisis and to get America's civil rights progress moving forward again. Of course this cannot be the only priority—we must also have well-managed industry, keep our farms productive, and make progress on environmental problems. But the management of schools and other public services must be one of America's priorities in the coming decades.

The measurement system involves a balanced look at student learning, using achievement test scores, especially growth rates, as well as parent/teacher surveys, participative management, and accountable school boards. While no system is perfect, these are solid indicators. They reveal substantial differences in performance, as much as two to one, between districts. One good measure can do more to improve performance than all the political rhetoric in the world. The concept of a year's growth for a year in school could do as much for education as yields per acre did for American farms or earnings per share did for business.

Of course, we need to be careful not to be too simplistic. Perhaps we can avoid some of the mistakes made in other fields—focusing too much on short-term results in business or not paying enough attention to the environment in both farms and factories. Applied nationally, these steps could add 3 to 4 years of productivity to the 12 years of public schooling in America. Taxpayers would really be getting their money's worth. The quality of life would be given a dramatic boost. Adequate salaries and funding for education would be justified. We would have a solid foundation for America's continued social progress and economic success in a postindustrial society and global economy of information and services.

To get these relatively simple measures applied to schools across the country, we must reach average citizens: parents, teachers, and taxpayers; young professionals, baby boomers, and older Americans. In a democracy the quality of public services depends on each of us, on how aggressive we are in the demands and expectations we enforce as consumers, and on how tough we are in insisting that reasonable standards be met. The practical, proven standards of performance, management, and accountability in this book give us something constructive and positive to be aggressive and tough about.

Armed with the right questions, and some idea of the right answers, average citizens can ask for growth rates and other key indicators, such as parent/teacher surveys. They can ask teachers if evaluation is really operational, fair, and effective, or just a facade. They can find out if their school board is really in charge and responsible to the public, or just a rubber stamp for superintendent authority.

7

Who: A Coalition of Citizens and Educators

Teachers should call for help from citizens. Those most likely to respond are the following:

- *Baby boomers* who are ready for social responsibility, for giving something back to the community, as America shifts from the "me" generation of the 1980s to more community and environmental concerns in the 1990s
- *Young professionals* who want public servants to be subject to the same expectations for performance and results that they experience in their own jobs, and who are anxious for their children to have the best possible education in a world of increasingly evident global economic competition
- *Older Americans* who launched the taxpayer revolt, questioning whether we are getting our money's worth from our investment in schools and other public services, and who understand that public services must be well managed if America's social progress and economic success are to continue.

Americans, young and old, have time for both personal success and social contribution. Our survival, and leaving enough of the American Dream for our children to enjoy, depend on our success in this. We cannot allow community and environment to deteriorate further. Most often it is not the motives that are missing but the techniques, an omission I hope this book will help to overcome.

We need a coalition of citizens and educators—parents, teachers, and students—to meet the needs of everyone, inside and outside the system (see Figure 2). Every American citizen has an interest in public affairs and the quality of our public services. You might see this in yuppies working with disadvantaged inner-city youths, or in retired

Figure 2
A Coalition of Citizens and Educators

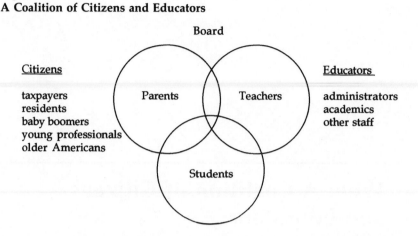

executives volunteering to help city schools. There is rising concern with community and environment, seen in the gentrification of our cities, cleaning up the environment, and media time devoted to public issues and concerns. Usually, however, media attention is limited to problems instead of solutions. Here we take that next step—not just theory or speculation but proven results and successful implementation.

A COALITION OF CITIZENS AND EDUCATORS

Several years ago the national PTA was a client of mine. In rummaging through their archives, I discovered that the original concept of the organization was broader and deeper than the idea that teachers and parents should talk together. It included the idea that you cannot totally separate the functions of parents and teachers with regard to children. Parents unavoidably function as the child's first and often most important teacher. Teachers often act in the role of parents. Of course teachers today are acutely aware of the added responsibilities they are often asked to shoulder from the parents' side of the equation. I have seen students put their arms around teachers or principals, asking for a hug in return, expressing a need for love that is not being fully met at home. Teachers and principals are admirably if often hopelessly struggling to meet these added demands.

Parents and teachers, citizens and educators, working together, can help drive forward the public management revolution to reach every school in our country. Teachers were able to use unions to win their freedom from traditional authoritarian school administration, but a broader concept of performance, management, and governance is needed to fill the vacuum. School board members have rightly asserted their responsibility to make sure that schools are competent, effective, and accountable—but they cannot do so by fighting teachers in contract negotiations and strikes. These two sides of the coin must be brought together if America's schools are to meet our needs for the future.

Both sides stand to benefit from effective school management: those who need good schools, and those who provide them. Neither side can do it alone. No matter how much parents might complain and get angry about city schools, they will never improve them without winning teachers over. And teachers will never get the funding they need for good schools and fair salaries without convincing parents that a good job is being done, that schools are accountable and effective. Thus a coalition is essential between

- The consumers of schools and other public services—citizens; students, parents, and taxpayers; baby boomers, young professionals, and older Americans concerned about the return on investment of their taxes, the quality of schools for their own children, or giving something back to the community

- Educators—broadly defined, those responsible for teaching our children in the classroom, administrators, board members, or other staff in the public schools or at colleges and universities.

The consumers of education have not been armed with practical standards. Yet in a democracy each of us is responsible for the quality of public services we receive. In some cases that quality has become so eroded that a crisis is at hand, evidenced by national deficits, overcrowded prisons, and the urban crisis. Citizens as consumers of public services cannot effectively voice their demands for quality without the standards of governance, management, and performance this book provides. Educators have too often overlooked management, failing to understand that it is the critical link between a productive staff and satisfied customers (students and parents). Knowing that teaching is the main driving force of education, they sometimes focus only on this, not realizing that the enabling management process is also essential. Some teachers have rejected or feared the factory model of management, borrowed from industry at the turn of the century, with an image of robber barons and top-down authority. They need to understand that management in industry has changed since the turn of the century, a time when schools borrowed administrative practices from industry.

During the ensuing decades, thanks partly to business schools and their application of the behavioral sciences, a much broader concept of performance, responsiveness to the customer, and job satisfaction and productivity for staff has evolved into the participative management now almost universal in professional, service, and managerial jobs. Teachers and unions have been busy winning freedom from authority; that is appropriate. But they have not yet taken the time to understand the concept or the specifics of participative, results-oriented management needed to replace traditional authoritarian school administration. Put aside secrecy and authority in favor of openness and freedom. Recognize the public need for accountability and proof of good performance. The combination is essential. Teachers need help from citizens in the following areas:

· To establish in each local school and district a system of participative and results-oriented management

· To replace traditional authoritarian school administration and the conflict and fragmentation of recent years with a new system of performance measures, participative management, and accountable boards

· To improve school performance by means of better management, ensuring that parents and students are well served, taxpayers are getting their money's worth, and the funding needed for good schools and fair salaries is justified.

CITIZENS

There is only one place to look for the leverage to achieve the quality schools we need for our future—America's citizens. We must all demand performance measures, participative management, and accountable boards. Democracy depends on public expectations, demands, and concerns. There is ample evidence of concern about school performance and management. But citizens also need a foundation for expecting and demanding the measurement and management techniques that are needed to produce good schools. A small group of leading school board members, administrators, and teachers—especially superintendents—have launched the public management revolution in schools. It is on their success that this book is based.

To reach schools across the country, and to extend the revolution to other public services, we must communicate this message to a larger audience. The following are the logical targets:

· Baby boomers

· Young professionals

· Older Americans and other taxpayers

· Parents

· Teachers

You do not have to measure and manage the schools yourself. You do need to know what questions to ask, and what answers to expect, to see if they are being measured and managed effectively by someone else.

Baby Boomers

Headed for their forties, baby boomers are reaching an age of readiness for community involvement: time to give something back to the community. Attitudes familiar from the 1960s—antiauthoritarian and prosocial justice—are reappearing among local school board members. Questioning the performance of schools, looking for a cause worthy of anger, something to really get excited about, the baby boomers could be a constructive force for changing America's schools. Without the Vietnam War and President Nixon, they need something else—a cause, a contribution, motivated by outrage and injustice.

The educational decline and urban crisis of America are our most serious moral failures of the twentieth century, threatening our national progress and success. Poorly performing public schools are causing the decline of America, saddling our nation with a frightening underdeveloped country in every big city, and limiting our ability to compete internationally. If these motivating forces could be turned to strengthening the performance and management of America's schools and public services, this would be the greatest contribution we could make to our continued social progress and future economic success. After years of self-help, it is time to give something back to the community. Anger and fear could be turned into hope and success.

Young Professionals

Anxious about the education of their children, perhaps because they have fewer, because of publicity about declining school performance, as an extension of their own ambition—for all these reasons young professionals want to evaluate and improve their local schools, to be sure they are up to par. They bring the performance and management standards of their jobs to education. Professionals in any field—research scientists, engineers, lawyers, doctors, accountants, consultants, those in health care, social services, and advertising, teachers in public schools, academics in higher education, corporate staff members—all have in common the desire for participative and supportive management, for autonomy and independence in decision making, and for measures of performance that separate outstanding contributors from average ones and that are used as a basis for compensation to reward development and improvement, encouraged (and funded) by the organization.

These are powerful experiences, and they are being made available to a growing proportion of our population. Most of us now work in services. Only 3 percent of Americans work on farms, and 25 percent in factories. The remainder—72 percent—are in services. Why tolerate lower standards of performance and management in schools and public services than in private services? Superintendents and principals have already noticed a change in the demands and expectations of young professionals for their children. They are more concerned about being sure that their children's educational experience is first-rate. Parents try to analyze the performance of schools in communities to which they may be moving. They recognize that the payoff from gentrification of cities will be held back unless poor urban schools are turned around.

If these people were equipped with appropriate standards for school performance and management, the expectations to which they are already subjecting schools would have a much more practical and positive impact.

Older Americans and Other Taxpayers

Contrary to some predictions, the tax protest in America has not died after its noisy beginning in California's Proposition 13 during the 1970s. Older Americans have the time and interest to convert their anger about taxes into a constructive contribution by applying standards of school performance and management. While the initial motive may be to find out if they are getting their money's worth, often there is a clear understanding that local property values depend on good schools. The objective is not to eliminate taxes, just to be sure there is a reasonable return on what is being invested.

And it is not just older Americans who are concerned about taxes. Young Republicans are equally anxious to improve the productivity of public services, and young Democrats to find more effective social services. Continued evidence of a taxpayer revolt in elections across the country reflects a wide range of ages and backgrounds.

Parents

Obviously parents have a strong interest in school performance and management. A limiting factor is the amount of time they have available. Many are already spending so much time on their jobs that few have the energy left to monitor school performance and management. Fortunately, only a few are needed. Those not obliged to work full time, or those with extra interest or energy, can assert the leadership needed to apply performance and management standards. It would be unrealistic to expect large numbers of parents to do this in a era of two-income families and single parents. But 1 percent would be enough. The stock market is kept honest by reporting of key financial indicators, subject to an outside audit. Financial experts analyze these data, keeping markets generally in a logical position and protecting those of us who lack the time and skill to carry out the analysis ourselves. The fact that someone is doing it benefits all of us. Published information need not be evaluated by every single investor in order to be useful to all. In the same way, a few parents in each district can give the leadership needed to apply performance and management standards to schools. All of us will benefit.

Teachers

Teachers can and must take a more active role in defining and implementing the new school governance, management, and performance concept. No one stands to win more from the public management revolution than do teachers: to be recognized as professionals contributing the most important function to a postindustrial and global economy of information and services, to participate more fully in management, to help schools become more responsive to their constituents, to achieve productivity improvements on a par with industry and agriculture, to prove that a good job is being done, and to justify fair salaries and adequate funding, recognition, and reward. Teacher unions have done a service by ending authoritarian administration in schools. But they have not yet made much of a contribution to defining the kind of management which should replace that tradition. The governance-management-performance system fills the gap.

I have helped to organize several conferences on school reform for teachers during the past few years. A high level of interest on the part of teachers in these issues and their desire to take an active role in debating them is evident. Every teacher speaking at these conferences has been in favor of teacher participation in school policy, governance, management, and reform. There is an enormous pool of untapped leadership talent in the teaching profession that could be released with the catalyst of a little instruction in modern requirements and successful techniques of school governance, management, and performance. That is what I would like to help teachers accomplish with this book.

There are many good reasons for teachers to be interested in a greater role in school governance, management, and performance. Most professional organizations are managed by those who come from and retain an active professional role: architectural, law, accounting, and consulting firms, for example. University administrators are usually chosen from academic ranks. Not far under the surface of every school administrator is a teacher, although the authoritarian tradition often made them seem on opposite sides of the street. I have had good results in consulting with school districts to develop organization concepts and intermediate-level positions straddling the traditional boundary between teachers and administrators, such as grade-level team leaders, coordinators in academic subject areas, and assistant principals.

Districts with a productive, positive relationship of teamwork, trust, and confidence among board, administration, and faculty are the most successful, in my experience. They work hard at a bottom-up style of management with communication in both directions, involving teachers directly in key decisions such as faculty recruitment and selection, curriculum and evaluation planning, and presentation of programs and results to the board.

Two things distinguish this approach from collective bargaining. First, a participative relationship with mutual responsibility for performance is assumed, rather than an adversarial or even combative relationship between board and staff. Second, performance information is used to prove where a good job is being done and to identify improvement opportunities. This provides a foundation for accountability to the public, for proving that taxpayers are getting their money's worth, and for justifying funding and salaries. The evaluation process and criteria, and objective information with the credibility of an outside audit, are key factors.

Pressures on schools and teachers today for accountability and improved performance are not so much criticism of the past as recognition of the growing importance of education and teaching. Teaching is on a rising curve, increasingly recognized as the most valuable function of a service economy. Education is the lever for success in a postindustrial society, the thing around which everything else turns, the source of momentum, the way society can move itself up the ladder of progress. America is increasingly recognizing how essential good schools are, not only to personal economic success but also to the economy of our urban communities, to keeping the cost of social services within limits we can afford, and to continuing our civil rights progress.

In the future, teachers will be to a global economy of information and services what capitalists were to the industrial revolution. Services, most of them public, are taking the place of industry as industry took the place of agriculture. One result is pressures on teachers and other public servants to improve performance. The rewards will be in better compensation where good performance is proven. There was a time when all value was thought to arise from the land; the landed gentry of Europe compensated themselves accordingly. Then there was a time when all value was said to arise from industry, and industrial executives justified their salaries and bonuses in this way. Increasingly we are recognizing that services are just as important, with adequate compensation needed to attract the talent and provide the recognition and reward needed to get the job done.

Justifying these salaries requires proof of responsibility for and delivery of good performance. This is the underlying social contract of the public management system recommended in this book. Managing education is the key to its productivity, just as management opened the door to productivity improvements in America's farms and factories. Only a few decades ago school management was the province of authoritarian superintendents and principals who had the authority to run schools without evaluation plans or the participation of teachers. The beginning of the end was clear with the advent of teacher unions.

Teacher empowerment is essential if educational performance is really to be improved. Teachers should understand and promote governance policies, performance measures, and management techniques that are fair and effective—improving performance, demonstrating that a good job is being done, and assuring positive support of teachers with recognition and reward for good performance. Teachers should insist on management that is fair to employees, productive for students and parents, and convincing to the board and public. This will enable teachers to capitalize on the rising tide of importance the public is placing on schools, and the rising allocation of resources, including salaries, that this can generate.

Too many teachers, especially those in America's big cities, are struggling to make an unmanaged system work effectively. Instead, they should be trying to change that system, not just to win more rewards for teachers but to prove through good performance achieved by good management that taxpayers are getting their money's worth, parents and community are satisfied, students are learning, and teachers are productive.

PUBLIC MANAGEMENT

The effectiveness of the organizations that serve us—both in helping the people they serve and in enhancing the productivity of their staff—depends on management. It is one of the most important functions of society, for our satisfaction as consumers and as employees, and for economic productivity and social well-being. Every responsible citizen, parent, teacher, and taxpayer should apply sound expectations and standards for good performance and results, and for job satisfaction and productivity of staff, to public services and to private enterprise.

As America shifts from the "me" generation of the 1980s to more concern with community and environment in the 1990s, the public management revolution beginning in the schools will gain momentum. Health care, housing, social services, and criminal justice will follow schools as the targets of Americans' scrutiny and reform.

Accomplishing positive change, however, will require a coalition. Neither the public nor the professionals responsible for these services can do it alone. Teamwork is needed to achieve a balance of accountability for citizens through participative management for staff. Therefore, all of us need to be armed with standards of performance and management for schools and public services, so our feelings of anger and concern can be turned to constructive action. We need to know what measures can be applied to schools, and what are reasonable standards of performance. We need a practical definition of participative management and performance-based planning, information, evaluation, and compensation in order to be able to tell if it exists in each of our schools and districts. And we need simple questions for our local board and superintendent, to see if accountability really exists. It is to meeting these needs that this book is dedicated.

8

Why: National Progress and Success, Urban Renewal and Civil Rights

Improving school performance will help to ensure America's continued social progress and economic success, including urban renewal and civil rights, with equal opportunity and economic competitiveness, in a global economy of information and services.

The positive implications of successful public schools, especially for our big cities, are enormous. Reforming our schools is the most important single step we can take to eliminate the risk of a permanent underclass. Good school performance is essential to keeping America competitive in the world economy. Good schools are the only affordable way we can address the problems of welfare, unemployment, criminal justice, and our national debt. While we must have these services, they are not very effective. It is impossible to fix these problems for most people once they become adults. But it is possible while they are still in school. It makes more sense to provide effectively managed schools than to try to solve the subsequent problems that poor schools produce.

Of course the lifetime achievement and satisfaction of these students is reason enough, apart from economic factors, for Americans not to tolerate poor performance in our schools.

THREE LEVELS OF BENEFITS

Perhaps the most important thing about school performance is that its benefits expand over time:

• From immediate results in learning, confidence, morale, and cost effectiveness

• To the lifetime achievement of students, and related social and economic implications, including the cost of social services and property values
• And finally to the long-run foundation for social progress and economic success.

Exhibit 5 outlines these three levels of impact, and the following paragraphs elaborate.

Current School Performance

The first level of performance is the immediate results achieved by the district in student learning and development, parent satisfaction and public confidence, teacher morale and job satisfaction, and cost-effectiveness. These indicators vary from one district to another, even in similar or neighboring communities: the combination can vary by as much as 20 to 1, each individual factor by as much as 2 to 1. One district is achieving 12 months of growth per year in student learning; another 6 months. One has parents and teachers 100 percent satisfied; another, only 50 percent. I have seen districts with similar IQ scores, in the 60s (in percentiles); but one has achievement test scores in the 70s and 80s while the other has achievement test scores in the 40s and 50s (again in percentiles).

Lifetime Student Achievement

These differences are multiplied in the lifetime achievement of students and related economic and social impacts. A child who learns to read before the distractions of puberty is equipped—not assured, but at least able—to move on to more important skills: writing, thinking, poetry, philosophy. A child who has not learned basic reading and math skills by puberty is apt to be distracted by other interests. From a humanistic point of view, the most important implication here is for the lifetime achievement, contribution, and quality of life for each individual. As fewer and less-well-paying jobs are available to those who lack the skills that a good education provides, these implications will become even more severe.

Another important factor at this level is the cost of social services such as welfare, unemployment, public housing, and criminal justice, including immediate costs, the high long-term cost of prisons, and the economic loss to the country from these individuals. Overspending on these services, which are not very productive or effective at best, has driven our national debt to alarming levels through budget deficits. The only affordable solution is good schools that reduce the need for these services to a level we can afford.

Exhibit 5
Three Levels of School Performance Impact

Participative and results-oriented management, board policies
of teamwork, and accountability and performance measures

↓

1. Current School Performance

— Student learning and development

— Parent satisfaction and public confidence

— Teacher morale and job satisfaction

— Cost-effectiveness

↓

2. Lifetime Student Achievement

— Personal quality of life, satisfaction, and achievement

— Implications for needed social services and related costs,
such as welfare, unemployment, public housing, and criminal
justice

— Local property values, dependent on good schools

— National deficits arising out of efforts to solve social problems
that are expensive, perhaps impossible, to solve after puberty

↓

3. National Progress and Success

— A foundation for America's economic success in a postindustrial
global society of information and services, where individual
competence and effectiveness will determine national economic
competitiveness

— Raising property values, encouraging urban renewal, eliminating
the underclass, and restarting America's civil rights progress.

Finally, local property values are dependent in part on good schools.
The potential for increasing real estate values in American cities is dramatic. In Europe, central city residential property values are several times those in the United States, and higher than similar property in European suburbs. The relationship is usually the opposite in America.

Here is an economic opportunity sufficient to whet the appetite of any yuppie.

National Progress and Success

The third level of impact is the most important: our national economic success and social progress. In the global competition of a world economy and a postindustrial society of information and services, education is the determining factor in economic competitiveness and success. It provides a solution to the problems of our cities by eliminating the underclass, encouraging urban renewal, and renewing civil rights progress. Our admirable civil rights accomplishments of the 1960s and 1970s seemed to stall in the 1980s; it does not help much to ride in the front of the bus if you cannot afford the fare. The door is open for upward mobility to America's minorities, but they will not be able to pass through it without the benefits of a good education, especially now, when many of the low-skill jobs previously available are no longer around. Those trying to break into the middle class today must have better skills and more education than our grandparents did.

IMPROVED PERFORMANCE AND RESULTS

The most important benefits of applying the public management revolution to schools are the improved performance and results that can be achieved and the benefits of these for individual Americans. Districts using the new system of governance, management, and performance with its emphasis on measuring results, participative management, and accountable school boards are achieving dramatic performance improvements:

- Student learning has increased an average of 37 percent in 10 research districts monitoring performance for 10–15 years.
- Increases measured by improvements in growth rates add as much as 3 to 4 more years of learning in 12 years of public schooling.
- Three urban communities have doubled the growth rate of student learning— from low single-digit levels like many big city schools—to double-digit growth rates equal to or better than suburban schools.
- Increases of 20–30 percent in growth rates of student learning have been achieved in every community that has applied the system.
- Suburban districts have added two to three years to the productivity of eight years' worth of investment in elementary schooling. Obviously these taxpayers are getting more for their money than they used to.

• These patterns are replicated in hundreds of schools and districts across the country.

The contribution of these students to our society and economy as a result of their improved learning performance is a contribution to our most important national resource—the talent and ability of our people. In addition, these schools have achieved improvements in confidence, satisfaction, morale, teamwork, and accountability. These academic achievements would provide a head start for American students that would benefit all of us, in every community and at every level of our society and economy.

SOCIAL PROGRESS AND ECONOMIC SUCCESS

Each generation faces a window of opportunity to solve the urban crisis, starting from the time each new class of students begins school. Once these children reach puberty, the distractions of modern life lead to high dropout rates for those who cannot read or write, to alarming numbers of teenage pregnancies and, for many, a life of crime, drugs, unemployment, and welfare.

Good schools mean even more to student development and potential success in cities than in the suburbs, where parents may be able to contribute more to their children's education.

Urban Children

In at least two important ways, the children of our cities need good schools today even more than the immigrants did. Negative family circumstances, television, drugs, and the sexual revolution are now being offset by hardworking teachers who know only too well that they are carrying a heavy load which used to be shared more equally with families and other social institutions.

At the same time, factory jobs that paid good money to people with little education are not as prevalent now; there will be even fewer in the future. This is not a failure of America; the rest of the world has just caught up with the advantages of industrialization. But this leaves the current residents of our cities without the kinds of jobs our grandfathers had: jobs that paid good money to those with little education. Instead, America's big city residents have to compete in a global economy of information and services, in which a good education is essential.

So schools today are even more important than they used to be, and teachers are being asked to carry a burden greater than that of their predecessors. Whether American education can meet this challenge will determine the economic and social progress of our country. As we enter an era of information and services, with industry declining in employment as agriculture did in the past, more and more of our economy is comprised of public services. Unless we find a way to manage them effectively, to achieve the same kind of productivity improvements that America showed the world in our farms and factories, the future will be one of decline.

Civil Rights, Urban Renewal, Economic Competitiveness

To solve the urban crisis, the only approach that can really work, and the only one we can afford, is investing in good schools (which do not cost any more than poor ones). City children can learn at rates equal to those of children in the suburbs, if they have good teachers and good schools. Good schools are the necessary foundation for America's continued economic prosperity in a global economy of information and services. The end of the class struggle is occurring as we realize that a well-educated work force is good for everyone, and essential to America's continued economic success in a global economy.

In order to get civil rights progress out of neutral gear, and ensure its advancement, we must add economic competitiveness to equal opportunity. Every person in America must be able to compete effectively for a job, in order to achieve personal success and national progress in a global economy of information and services. This is the answer to improving the quality of America's life—not more money spent on fighting crime, not more prisons or welfare, but making every American educationally able to be economically competitive in a world economy.

Good schools would raise property values in every American community, especially in major cities, where values are artificially depressed by poor schools (compared with major European cities, where the highest residential property values are in city centers).

A permanent underclass is like having a Third World country in the middle of each of our big cities. The cost of public services is becoming unaffordable, with continuing and mounting federal deficits. Self-help is not enough; we must have effective public services. Teamwork and community spirit are needed to solve the problem of how to make public services effective, to get America's progress and success moving forward again.

The public management revolution beginning in schools, and improved school performance, will accomplish the following:

• Make America competitive again is the postindustrial world—a global economy of information and services

- Put a new and solid foundation under the progress of individual prosperity in America
- Rekindle America's civil rights progress by adding economic competitiveness to equal opportunity
- Support urban renewal, and raise urban property values to finance it
- Eliminate the underclass
- Reduce the need for and cost of prisons, welfare, unemployment, and social services
- Solve the dilemma of federal deficits
- Refocus America's attention on domestic progress now that the Cold War is ending
- Provide a practical, positive model for effective reform of all public services.

SCHOOL PERFORMANCE IMPROVEMENTS

If the measurement and management system described in this book were applied in every American school and district, we would achieve a full year's growth annually everywhere. This would raise performance in many suburban and rural districts. It would turn around results in America's city schools, many now achieving only a few months of growth for a year in school. This would be the most valuable contribution we could make to the children of our cities, and to our nation's most pressing social and economic problems: reducing the underclass, giving America the trained workers we need for global competition, and containing the cost of domestic social services within limits we can afford.

But more than just school performance is at stake. The public management revolution beginning in schools could—with your help—give America the educated citizens we need for the future. It could lead to dramatic productivity improvements in all public services, comparable with those of our farms and factories earlier. This will drive America's continued progress and success into the twenty-first century.

SATISFACTION AND RESULTS

The main characteristic of the revolution is to measure public services by results, with proof of good performance; a quality product measured, where possible, with customer and staff satisfaction, responsiveness to people, and understanding of their needs and desires. Applied in schools, this public management concept results in a performance-driven system of policies, plans, and measures, with good performance justifying funding and salaries. The concept is equally needed in and applicable to other public services: health care, justice, and social services, for example.

PUBLIC MANAGEMENT REVOLUTION

The potential impact of this system on the productivity of schools and other public services is so dramatic that I have called it a public management revolution. The public management revolution beginning in schools could make as great a contribution to America's productivity, prosperity, progress, and success as the industrial and agricultural revolutions. This third phase of American progress and reform will see education recognized as a critically important function in a postindustrial society, as a way that we can move ourselves up the ladder of progress.

Now that the Cold War is winding down, America is returning to complete the Progressive reform that began at the turn of the twentieth century. The focus this time will shift from business and agriculture to public services. Better management in public services will contribute as much to our society and economy as industry and agriculture did earlier. Improving the quality of America's education, health, and government services will be the primary source of our economic growth and social progress in the twenty-first century. In spite of the continuing importance of agriculture and industry, further progress in human productivity, driven first by agriculture and second by industry, must now be driven by productivity improvements in public services.

9

How: Measurement, Management, and Accountability

Here are three specific steps to apply performance measures, participative management, and board accountability in your schools. In a few hours, armed with these three questions, you can assess the accountability of your local school board and superintendent; evaluate management to see whether the modern, participative, results-oriented style has reached your school yet; and begin to measure performance. The key is knowing what questions to ask and what answers to expect. With these guidelines, you will be able to find out whether your schools are coping successfully with the new management requirements, or still lingering in the authoritarian era of conflict and decline. You can do this from outside the system, as a citizen, taxpayer, or parent, or from inside, as board member, administrator, teacher, or student.

Management consultants look at any organization as a system to be evaluated by how well it functions. Sometimes you are obliged to do this quickly, other times you have weeks or months to fill in the details. In either case, a few key questions, tailored to the character of performance and management in a specific institution, are critically important. From my experience, these are the questions for schools:

• Is your school measured?
• Is your district managed?
• Is your board accountable?

YOU CAN BE A MANAGEMENT CONSULTANT

There are two things that I have found especially rewarding about management consulting, the reasons I have stayed in the field for 25 years. One is the perspective of what is going on in the world and how things work, a little like that enjoyed by a sociologist, but with more immediate involvement in the events and problems of the world today. Second is the satisfaction of helping to solve these problems.

This chapter explains the criteria I have used as a management consultant to assess school systems—the three steps you can take to evaluate and improve your schools:

1. Performance information to measure results
2. Management process for positive support of teachers and administrators
3. Board policy for teamwork and accountability.

The questions are discussed below.

Performance—Is Your School Measured?

Ask the superintendent for growth rates. Expect a year's growth for a year in school in each subject, grade, and school. Growth rates are calculated by, for instance, subtracting last year's fourth grade achievement test score from this year's fifth grade score (using any of the major national tests). A common range of performance is zero to two years. Districts should publish their growth rates.

Are parents, teachers, and students regularly surveyed to identify satisfaction and improvement opportunities?

Are student learning/test data analysis and parent/teacher surveys subject to an outside audit?

Management—Is Your District Managed?

Ask teachers if they are evaluated. When unions ended traditional authoritarian school administration abruptly in the 1960s, most districts stopped evaluating teachers. Well-managed districts have participative, results-oriented teacher evaluation and administrative compensation based on performance.

Is your district responsive to parents and teachers, with participation, communication, teamwork, trust, and confidence?

Are all principals paid the same salary, with the same annual increase, or is compensation based on performance, with different salaries and increases for each?

Governance—Is Your Board Accountable?

Ask the board if the superintendent reports evaluations to them. Traditionally, superintendents treated boards with the same authority they used
on the staff. Modern superintendents report evaluation process and
results to the board, so they can judge performance on behalf of the
public.

Does your board have understandable test data analysis and parent/teacher
surveys with an outside audit?

Does your board have policies (and practices) of teamwork, responsiveness,
and participation?

Armed with these guidelines, you will be able to find out whether
your schools are coping successfully with the new management requirements of schools, or still lingering in the authoritarian era of conflict and decline. When evaluating your school, remember that schools
have only recently come into an era of new management requirements,
so no one has had a long period of time to meet them successfully.
Superintendents today can still remember the autocratic style that was
employed through the 1950s and into the 1960s, and that still exists in
many districts.

The first district to move in this direction was in the small town of
Lake Forest, Illinois, north of Chicago, in 1972. Other districts have
learned from Lake Forest's experience and/or invented their own responses to common requirements for a more participative and results-
oriented style.

The transition will not occur overnight. It could easily take a year or
two to put into place the management systems, and several years more
to achieve the potential performance improvements. And you will have
to bring along virtually the entire staff of the district to understand the
change. Does it sound challenging? Yes, but it can be done.

YOU CAN DO IT

Will America have the schools and public services it needs? It all
depends on you. If you just sit back and criticize the poor quality of
American schools and public services, you will have plenty to complain
about. But if you are willing to understand the questions—and answers—you can make a real and positive contribution to quality.

Management is the determining factor in the performance of any organization. Progress in school performance in districts that have recognized and met these requirements is startling. They have leaped ahead
by as much as three to four years of achievement, doubling rates of

student learning in some cases, with equally substantial improvements in parent and teacher satisfaction, public confidence, and taxpayer willingness to support the expenditures needed to achieve good schools. These districts follow the pattern summarized in this chapter and explained in the rest of the book:

· Performance is measured using simple, practical techniques:
  —A year's growth for a year in school
  —Parent and teacher satisfaction measured by surveys
  —Cost-effectiveness through rigorous analysis of key factors
  —Objective accuracy through an outside audit

· Teachers and administrators are treated with respect:
  —Communication, participation, teamwork, trust, and confidence
  —Performance-based evaluation and compensation, with positive support for improvement
  —Recognition and reward for good performance

· School boards have a solid basis for accountability:
  —Objective information indicating student learning and parent/teacher satisfaction
  —Evaluation process and results reported to the board
  —Superintendent selected and evaluated on the basis of performance measures and participative management.

If you could bring along your school and district in this direction, America's students could advance educationally by as much as 3 to 4 years during the 12 years of public schooling. Students could achieve as much by the age of 14 or 15 as they do now by 17 or 19. The easing of our national problems of the underclass, civil rights, urban decline, and economic competitiveness would be substantial. America's progress and success into the twenty-first century would be assured. You could be confident that the schools in your local community were good enough for your children, that local taxpayers are getting their money's worth, that America's property values and economic competitiveness, as well as social progress and civil rights, rest on a sound basis.

You do not have to measure the school yourself, or to manage it. You do need to know the right questions to ask—and the right answers to expect—to find out if it is being measured and managed. This chapter presents three questions to ask when evaluating your school, and their answers. Alone, it will give you a quick impression of performance, management, and accountability in your district. The last four parts of the book complete the questions and supporting detail, so you can compare your district's performance, management, and accountability with the best—and worst—that I have seen in 15 years of experience in hundreds of schools.

The contribution you will make to your community by identifying improvement opportunities and bringing them to the attention of your school board will be substantial. You might find a well-managed, high-performance district. More likely, you will find one that is not yet well managed, and that is not performing as well as it could.

As we apply these standards to schools across the country, and similar standards to other public services, we will be able to reestablish America's economic success and restart our social progress. This could be America's greatest accomplishment in the coming century, equaling what we did in industry and agriculture in earlier eras. I hope you can make a contribution to this important development.

PERFORMANCE INFORMATION

Unique to the governance, management, and performance system described in this book is the emphasis on measuring performance. Woodrow Wilson first distinguished between policy and administration in public affairs almost a century ago. That distinction remains one of the cornerstones of public management in America, and rightly so. Adding a third level to this historic dichotomy may seem a bold assertion, but my experience convinces me that it is right. When I began to analyze the problems of local government in England in the late 1960s and early 1970s, I could see that each local government was in a hundred different businesses, none of them well-defined or well-measured. Although setting objectives was one logical answer, one that we tried and one I still believe is necessary, in the end it was disappointing.

Objectives often proved, after long political debate, to be mere platitudes. When we could find something that could really be measured, dramatic progress was made. By consolidating social services into one department, for example, we could allocate the funds saved by not putting a child into an orphanage to other social services that might be the ones needed to enable a child to remain at home. Supporting cooking and housekeeping services, for example, might enable a grandparent to care for the child. In the housing area, a figure of 37 percent inadequate housing galvanized action in a massive program that lowered the figure to 17 percent in less than a decade, and justified the investment of huge sums needed to accomplish this.

In schools, many of the most important components of the basic mission of learning are measurable. We are fortunate to have well-developed, established, proven achievement tests. Of course they do not measure everything, and the numbers change frequently, especially if you look at individual children or small groups. But when you consider schools and districts, these numbers are reliable, and they measure things that are important. You should recognize, however, that they do not measure many of the more important objectives of schools, or human development. When you look at these numbers, as we will in some detail, you will see that a reasonable expectation is a year's growth for a year in school. Some of the districts I have worked with were achieving only half this much. By hard work, evaluation, and aggressive recruitment they were able to attract and retain a staff that could produce twice as much. That is what we need to do in many of our big city schools.

As a result, students in these districts are now achieving as much by the age of 10 as they had been by the age of 14. That is the kind of jump we can achieve with good schools. I do not mean we want our children growing up faster, but we do want to give them the basic skills to be successful in the world at the earliest age we reasonably can. Many of our students could do this earlier than they do now, and they would then surprise us by how much more they can accomplish later. Many districts are already achieving these good results. And this will not take slow, disadvantaged students and put them automatically in the same league as bright students from families whose nurturing and stimulation are advantages that cannot be replaced. But it does mean that students in every school can achieve a year's growth for a year in school. In fact, on this standard, students who start out behind have more room to grow than those who start out ahead. A district with disadvantaged students has more room to show growth than one with advantaged students. This demonstrates the greater importance of teachers, compared with families and circumstances, in communities with disadvantaged students. Whether that greater value should be matched by higher salaries is something you can think about for yourself.

The second technique is simple market research: asking consumers and staff. This is comparable with what business learns by analyzing sales figures to see if anyone is buying the product. In schools, this requires simple, straightforward questionnaires addressed to parents, teachers, and students. The most useful information comes from parents and teachers in the early years of schooling, and from students in later years. Measuring results must not detract from the important things school do that cannot be measured. My recommendation in those areas is not even to try. "Great books" discussions as early as the third grade (one of Mortimer Adler's recommendations) seem to me a marvelous idea that ought to be available to every child in America. The motivation to read may well be more important than the mechanical details of how to do so. Understanding of poetry and philosophy is not measured by tests. Still, we must have students who achieve the basic skills at the earliest age they reasonably can. And we must have schools which accomplish that mission. If this is not done by the age of puberty, remedial efforts later on will be expensive, and disappointing.

You may be surprised that school districts do not routinely use surveys and analyze test scores. Remember that historically the superintendent's job was to keep such sensitive performance information secret, to keep the board happy without revealing such details of performance, much as business managers used to keep the public in the dark about profits and other results. Educators have been accustomed to working without sharp measures of performance; it often does not seem right to them that this should change. You are very likely to find districts in which test scores exist, but are presented in a way that no one can understand. In some cases test company sales may actually benefit from results that cannot be understood, since districts can then say they are testing without actually revealing results.

MANAGEMENT PROCESS

When you look at the management process in your district, expect to find someone assessing the situation and needs in each school and department, taking responsibility for performance, and setting reasonable objectives to move in the right direction. Here are two practical examples:

• A new principal takes over a school that has proven somewhat difficult in years past because it is a little further from the center of town than other schools in the district, and the community has a tendency to be somewhat fragmented. The new principal's major challenge in the current year, as a young woman replacing a veteran of 20 years, is to take charge successfully, especially in relationships with parents, teachers, and students.

• A new director of the physical education department in a high school is taking over for a husband-and-wife team who had not developed an equal distribution of opportunities between boys and girls, and who had allowed some older faculty members to work a light schedule. The challenge is to modernize and turn around the department.

The second component of an accountability system is performance information, which has already been discussed. Once the information is available, it must be analyzed and used positively to build confidence, provide positive reinforcement, and improve performance. You should be careful that calculating and processing information does not cost too much relative to its value.

The third component is fair and effective evaluation for both teachers and administrators. Probably the most important factor here is that the system is really operational. I have hardly ever been in a school system that did not have a plan on paper, but the number operational is a small fraction of those which exist on paper.

Please do not misunderstand this: no profession is perfect. Teachers and administrators, like performers in every field, are not always up to standard. Someone needs to assess this and take action. In most big city school districts it has been 20 to 30 years since any administrator or teacher was really evaluated. If you have a district without recent evaluation, you have undoubtedly accumulated some low performers. From my personal experience in serving on the school board in Lake Forest, even a well-managed, high-performance district loses about 1 teacher out of 100 each year. If that 1 percent loss rate were allowed to accumulate for 20–30 years, you can see that, even with the pressures on poor teachers to leave the system voluntarily, you could easily accumulate 10–20 percent inadequate performers. Inadequate teaching may well be concentrated in some schools rather than spread evenly across all. You can see the potential impact on performance that this could, and does, have.

Performance-based compensation for administrators is a must. This has also been successfully applied to teachers. It is a simple plan of categories, targets, and ranges that involves a basic trade-off on the part of the school board: teamwork in exchange for accountability. This in turn requires performance-based compensation, information, and evaluation, and relationships of trust and confidence. Performance-based compensation is worthless without performance information; do not buy a system that fails to follow through with documented evidence of good performance. Do not start with merit pay for teachers. You will have to meet the other management requirements outlined in this book, especially those for teamwork, trust, and confidence, and for fair and effective evaluation, before you can even consider merit pay. Otherwise merit pay will be like unclogging your kitchen sink with dynamite. You will get a reaction, but it will be a little messier than you expected, as many well-intentioned school boards have found.

BOARD POLICY AND SUPERINTENDENT LEADERSHIP

The single most powerful step that any school board can take toward performance measures and management plans is to evaluate the superintendent on this basis. By insisting that the superintendent develop and implement a management process and provide simple, understandable performance information, school boards can ensure that America moves in the direction of well-managed, high-performance school. If they do not take these steps, we will get there anyway, but it will take much longer, and your district may never make it.

As you apply these criteria to your own district, remember that there is more than one way to be successful. Smaller districts do not need as formal a management or performance information system as larger ones. However, they require the same basic components. Remember, too, that there is need for judgment in education: it is inherently difficult to measure. There is an emotional intensity required in teaching children that must be taken into account. Be sensitive to the needs of teachers for encouragement and support.

Not even the best teacher can succeed with every child. Students grow in fits and starts. Do not expect every student to advance the same amount every year, or every classroom to perform the same as any other. Do expect satisfied parents, teachers, and students, and evidence of learning: a year's growth for a year in school from every classroom and school in your system. These are the basics of good school performance. Then you can go on to loftier objectives such as poetry, philosophy, advanced programs in language and math, music, art, drama, sports, and other programs that for many students are the basic connection between school and the world.

Armed with the questions and answers in this chapter, you can assess the level of board accountability, participative management, and performance measurement in your district right now. However, to really give you the tools you need—to know what to ask for, to know what a sound management plan looks like, to know what performance measures are, how they actually work, and the actual results achieved in districts of various types, with specific steps and criteria for evaluating the superintendent and board—the rest of this book condenses my 15 years of experience in evaluating and improving schools. I present measurement and management plans, and results I use in evaluating the schools that I work with as a management consultant.

Most districts are still in the early stages of a transition that requires many years to complete successfully. But you should expect your district to recognize these new requirements and at least to be moving conscientiously and as quickly as reasonable to meet them.

I hope you use these questions to join the public management revolution beginning in schools, and that you find them helpful in strengthening your contribution to evaluating and improving the performance of your local schools.

IV

The System: Governance,
Management, and
Performance

10

Overview: The Governance-Management-Performance System

This chapter provides an overview of the governance-management-performance system. This new concept of school management—emphasizing people and results—can be expressed in three words:

Governance means board policies and superintendent leadership for teamwork and accountability.

Management involves communication, evaluation, and compensation, with support systems for teachers and administrators.

Performance requires measures of results, such as student learning and parent/teacher satisfaction.

Good school performance is achieved through teamwork at three levels: governance, management, performance; board, administrators, teachers; policies, techniques, measures. The governance-management-performance concept is implemented through a participative and accountable management system that organizes planning and evaluation around solid information: analysis of student learning using test data, and parent/teacher satisfaction using surveys. This provides a sound basis for performance-based compensation, fair evaluation, and teamwork.

Thousands of teachers, administrators, and board members are already achieving effective schools. By using this model, they have communication and participation, positive management, accountable boards, motivated staffs, satisfied parents, a confident public—and more learning.

Exhibit 6 summarizes the system.

Exhibit 6
The Governance-Management-Performance System

1. *Governance:* Policies and leadership for teamwork and accountability

   • Standards of governance, management, and performance applied on behalf of the community
   • The superintendent selected and evaluated on this basis
   • Reports of evaluation process and results to the board
   • Participative management with teamwork, support, communication, and responsiveness
   • Performance measures with outside audit

2. *Management:* Participative management, emphasizing communication and performance

   • Well-defined organization, responsibility, and relationships
   • Communication, participation, teamwork, trust, and confidence
   • Performance-based planning, organization, information, evaluation, development, and compensation
   • Positive reinforcement, support, development, recognition, and reward for staff
   • Responsiveness to needs and desires of parents, students, taxpayers, and citizens

3. *Performance:* Pragmatic measures of learning, confidence, morale, and cost

   • Student learning and development
   • Public confidence and parent satisfaction
   • Teacher morale and job satisfaction
   • Cost-effectiveness
   • Outside audit
   • Used for positive reinforcement, to justify funding, build confidence, and improve performance

STRATEGY FOR TEAMWORK AND SUCCESS

In successful school districts, more humane and participative management, emphasizing people and results, is replacing traditional school administration and conflict. This participative style underlies America's democracy, the foundation for our world leadership. It is time to apply it to schools.

The second major theme is more attention to measurements of results. Practical application of the scientific method was the foundation for the agricultural and industrial revolutions. Its impact on the world in so many ways, including the behavioral sciences, has been tremendous—but it has not yet affected most public services.

As a result of these innovations, applied in a strategy of teamwork and success, significant improvements are being achieved in learning, satisfaction, and cost.

A PERFORMANCE-DRIVEN SYSTEM

Performance is a component that must be added to the traditional American public administration concept. It provides feedback and objective data to the governing board. It encourages board and staff to focus on defining mission and purpose. In the language of corporate planning, this is equivalent to defining what business you are in.

The result is a performance-driven school system, which has advantages for teachers, administrators, board members, students, parents, and taxpayers. For teachers, it offers more job satisfaction, and justification of the funding needed for good schools and fair salaries. For administrators, it justifies positions and salaries based on responsibility for performance. For school boards, it is a positive, practical basis for accountability, and makes their job easier, allowing attention to be directed toward more important issues and decisions, instead of time and effort being wasted in conflict. For students, parents, and taxpayers, it provides better performance in learning, satisfaction, and cost-effectiveness. For America, it supports economic development, property values, and civil rights.

The three key components—performance, management, and governance—are summarized in the rest of this chapter.

Performance

One key implementation step for the new school governance, management, and performance system is to measure performance.

Student Learning. A year's growth for a year in school is a standard that anyone can apply and every school can achieve. It encourages a focus of attention on the fundamental purpose of schools: student learning.

Parent Satisfaction. Parent surveys encourage responsiveness to meeting customer needs and desires, and provide one key indication of results.

Teacher Satisfaction. A teacher survey stresses the importance of staff participation and job satisfaction. Asking teachers what they think also encourages a more open, humane, and participative style of management.

Triangulating the three indicators provides reassurance in focusing on priorities. Typically parent and teacher survey results show a high degree of consistency. Students and taxpayers often agree.

Of course this formula is not a perfect or complete representation of school performance. It focuses on the basics. Much as people first seek to meet their needs for food and shelter, and then turn to a higher objective, so basic skills are building blocks that all students need.

Management

Naturally, with so much public and legislative attention focused on school reform, every board is interested in accountability. In some districts, board concern has become a problem, eroding traditional support for administrators, especially compared with the protection teachers have obtained through unions.

The heart of successful implementation is a practical, proven system to hold administrators responsible for performance, and to reward them accordingly. This system has been successfully implemented in scores of districts with hundreds of schools and thousands of administrators. It has been used across the country, through my personal consulting and books.

The system includes the following:

- Board accountability, teamwork, and support
- Fair and effective administrative evaluation
- Administrative compensation using categories, targets, and ranges
- Evaluation criteria and procedures for categorizing positions
- Comparative administrative salary data
- Procedures for the board to evaluate administrative performance.

This part of the system might be compared to the drive train in your car. You need each of the component parts—planning, information, evaluation, and compensation—including the mechanics of categories, targets, and ranges, in order to make the system work. With common sense, anyone can understand the system. It is challenging to implement, however, because it involves connecting board and staff through the leadership of the superintendent and management team.

Governance

Board policies and superintendent leadership are both the most and the least important part of the three levels of action needed: least important because none of the actual work of the school is done here; most important because this is the level of highest potential leverage for improved performance.

If school board members—and those active citizens, both taxpayers and parents, in each community who watch school boards—would evaluate their local board and superintendent using the performance and management standards in this book, the positive contribution to the quality of American schools would be enormous. By building confidence in public schools, proving where a good job is being done, realistically identifying improvement opportunities, and actually improving performance, an upward spiral of performance, confidence, and support is generated. This helps to justify the funding we need for good schools and fair salaries, and provides continuing, positive reinforcement to sustain ongoing performance improvements.

You can achieve similar results by applying the system in your school and district.

11

Performance: Pragmatic Measures of Progress and Results

Measuring performance is the most important and cost-effective step to improvement. Pragmatic measures can have the same positive impact on school performance as the scientific method did on agriculture and industry. The formula for measuring schools is

$$\frac{\text{Learning} \times \text{Confidence} \times \text{Morale}}{\text{Cost}}$$

Each component of the outside audit school performance formula is defined in Exhibit 7.

Learning is measured by analysis of achievement and ability, with emphasis on growth. Careful, positive analysis and use of information are essential: percentiles of achievement and ability, grade equivalents and growth rates for district, school, classroom, and students. Obviously learning is the main purpose of schools; while these measures are imperfect, they focus on mission and purpose, with positive reinforcement for staff, a powerful motivation for improvement.

Another important category of information is feedback from key constituents: students, parents, teachers, graduates, taxpayers, and community. Simple, straightforward, hard-hitting performance questions help set priorities and differentiate between schools, classrooms, subjects, and services where there is high satisfaction and those where there are realistic improvement opportunities. Using these criteria, performance varies remarkably even between similar, neighboring schools and districts:

Exhibit 7
The Outside Audit School Performance Formula

$$\frac{\text{Learning} \times \text{Confidence} \times \text{Morale}}{\text{Cost}}$$

Learning: student learning and development, measured by test scores (growth rates and other indicators)

Confidence: parent satisfaction and public confidence, measured by surveys

Morale: teacher morale and job satisfaction, also measured by surveys

Cost: expenditures to achieve these results

• A typical range of student learning performance is from zero to two years of growth per year in school.

• Constituent satisfaction varies in a range of about 50 percent to 100 percent.

WHY MEASURE RESULTS?

We need pragmatic measures for schools and other public services like those which led to America's success in agriculture and industry—proof that a good job is being done, identifying improvement opportunities, justifying salaries and budgets. Within the governance-management-performance system, perhaps the most important factor is the need to measure results, using a realistic, measurable concept of school performance that focuses attention on basic purposes and provides a framework for planning. Test scores, even with their inherent limitations, encourage a strong and appropriate focus on student learning. Surveys encourage a more humane and participative style of management, responsive to customers and staff.

A concept and measures of performance focus attention on defining and achieving mission and purpose. Public and board confidence requires key performance indicators. Performance information puts a solid foundation under board accountability, with an outside audit to ensure objectivity, analytical experience, and comparisons. By measuring results from the bottom up, an emphasis on customer and staff satisfaction and student learning is reinforced. Performance responsibilities are more clearly defined. Important and realistic improvement opportunities are identified. Consideration is concentrated on the central question of what business you are in, what results are needed, and what is being achieved.

BACKGROUND

I first realized the need for measures of public services when I shifted from corporate business planning to working with local governments in England. I discovered there were no measures of what business they were in, let alone how they were doing in it, whether customers were satisfied, and whether the amount of services being provided had some reasonable relationship to the level of need. Applying these lessons when I first began working with public schools in the United States in 1973 led me to search hard for things that could be measured. I found a well-developed testing industry. It grew out of the same tradition that gave us the Army Alpha and Beta tests which helped America win World War I by enabling us to base assignments and promotions on merit rather than on the European tradition of social class—an admirably American outlook. The four major testing companies had extended this deeply into the school arena.

I looked in some detail at the extent to which these tests were accurate and reliable. At least for basic skills, they measured up very well. If students did not have the basic skills by the time of puberty, the distractions in today's society often meant that they never did get them. So measuring basic skills seemed important. Combined with the fact that some districts were achieving so much more student growth than others, the implications seemed clear. Later, I began to see districts in urban communities achieving more than a full year's growth for a year in school. The implication: our big cities can do the same. All we have to do is raise our standards in these big cities, measure results, hold the results up to these standards, and then ask administrators and teachers to run faster until they get up to reasonable speed.

I appreciate that this is oversimplified, and I recognize that teachers in cities are dealing with difficult problems, but if it is possible to achieve a year of learning for a year in school, that is what we have to do.

Beyond test scores, I found that very simple techniques of market research applied to schools could provide extremely valuable feedback from parents, teachers and other staff members, students, and graduates. This feedback is as valuable as, perhaps even more valuable than, market research or sales data in a company. Surveys also tend to balance test scores, which have a rather sharp edge, with softer opinions and impressions.

Of course judgment about performance of a district, school, classroom, or student is necessarily subjective. It cannot be reduced to any single number, or even to a formula with several factors. That is what school boards, superintendents, principals, and teachers are there for. Their judgment must carry the most weight. But, as with our public companies, we consumers and investors need some simple statistics like sales, profits, earnings per share, and return on investment. We need to have those statistics confirmed by an independent outside source so that we can depend on their reliability, accuracy, and comparability. We need to be guided in interpreting them by someone with experience in looking at more than one district. And we need to be sure that our local school boards and administrators are considering these data.

After all, would you buy stock in a company whose board did not understand earnings per share? Who did not monitor that statistic closely? Who did not watch sales data? Who did not know if the company was making a profit? Of course not. But you may well be putting your children in schools or paying taxes to a district in which the school board does not know the growth rate of student learning or the percentage of satisfied parents and teachers. In the business community, measuring results includes financial and sales analysis and all other analytical techniques that business—with the help of business schools, management consultants, and others—has developed and applied. Public services for the most part have not attempted this kind of analysis. The value lies not only in measuring results but also in defining purposes so that results can be measured. The whole process can have an enormous positive impact on productivity.

Obviously, performance information is critically important. It also needs to be verified by an outside audit. In schools, the focus should be on student learning, which is to a useful extent (but not completely) indicated by test data. And parent/teacher satisfaction should be measured through surveys. Other indicators are also useful, but generally not as important as these key factors. Costs, attendance, dropout and discipline statistics, and a variety of other indicators also need to be reviewed. Not all of the purposes and accomplishments of schools can be measured, but that is no reason not to measure what can be measured.

Exhibit 8 summarizes benefits and results of the outside audit school performance formula. Applying the formula produces a performance range between a high of 20 and a low of 0. The worst school evaluated showed no growth at all. The best achieved 20 months of growth, compared with a national average of 10. With high levels of parent and teacher satisfaction and low cost, this school achieved an overall score of 20.

A management process is also needed: communication, participation, teamwork, trust, and confidence on the one hand, and performance-based planning, information, evaluation, and compensation on the other. A final and critically important, but relatively small, ingredient is board insistence on performance measures and participative management. Without strategic direction at this level, neither is likely to occur.

Exhibit 8
The Outside Audit Concept for Schools

Participative and results-oriented management replaces traditional authoritarian administration and conflict and adds a third level of performance measures to the classic American distinction between policy and administration in public affairs.

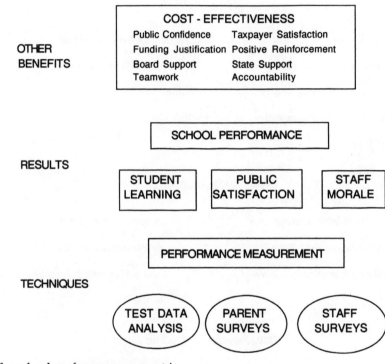

The school performance concept is

- Student learning and development
- Parent satisfaction and public confidence
- Teacher morale and job satisfaction
- Cost-effectiveness and administrative procedures

RESULTS

The results of applying this governance-management-performance system are substantially improved student learning, parent satisfaction and public confidence, teacher morale and job satisfaction, and overall district cost-effectiveness. More humane and participative relationships within the organization and with its constituents are also important. An upward spiral of positive reinforcement can be just as powerful as the negative spiral that we have witnessed in our big cities in the past few decades, and is obviously more desirable.

To illustrate performance differences, following is an outline of the contrast of high and low performance that I have personally observed.

Low Performance   High Performance

Learning Growth Rates

Growth rates of student   Learning growth rates of as

learning as low as zero in   much as two years for a year in

individual schools, and as   school

low as six months in entire

districts

Achievement vs. Ability

A district with achievement   A district with ability

percentiles in the 50s and   percentiles in the 50s

ability percentiles in the 60s   and achievement percentiles

                                           in the 80s

Improvement vs. Decline

Declining achievement and   Rising percentiles of

ability percentiles as children   achievement and ability

move from first grade to high   as children progress from

school   the first grade to high school

Satisfaction

Levels of constituent *   Constituent * satisfaction as

satisfaction as low as 50 percent.   high as 100 percent.

* Parents, teachers, students, graduates and taxpayers.

CONCLUSIONS

What do these performance differences mean, and what should we do about them? I have reached the following conclusions:

- Some taxpayers are getting twice as much for their money as others. Local property values are varying by at least as much as a result.
- Learning rates vary from nothing to as much as 2 years for a year school. Some districts are achieving 10–12 years of learning for 8 years of school, and others are achieving only 4–6 years. Parent, teacher, student, graduate, and taxpayer satisfaction shows similar wide variation.
- Particularly when you consider the impact of puberty on students who may find it more satisfactory to disguise their inability to read, the personal implications of these students are dramatic: improvement of their employment prospects; ability to compete; dependence on welfare, unemployment, and other social services; likelihood of being involved in the criminal justice system; and personal ability, development, achievement, and success.
- In an age when well-paying jobs are no longer available for those without education, the economic implications are saddening, yet the opportunity to turn around the situation with education is encouraging.
- Urban students can succeed. The opportunities for increasing property values and eliminating the underclass, especially in our big cities, are exciting. The cost of welfare, crime, and unemployment could be contained and national deficit spending eliminated. Civil rights would be advanced, perhaps even more effectively through economic competitiveness than they were through equal opportunity. Instead of the disadvantaged being further handicapped by poor educations, they would be given a corresponding advantage through productive schools.
- Management makes the difference; well-managed schools can perform effectively in communities of all kinds. The need is for performance measures, participative management, and accountable boards.

RECOMMENDATIONS

What to do? Here are my suggestions for action.

- Start by measuring learning in your school using growth rates (see Chapter 17).
- Follow this with surveys of parents and teachers (see Chapters 15 and 16).
- Look for a few key indicators to see if your district is effectively managed with participation of teachers, mainly by asking teachers and administrators about evaluation, communication, and teamwork.
- Check to be sure your board is accountable: Are they insisting upon the three steps listed above?
- Begin with the schools in your community, using the criteria in this book,

and then extend the concept of measurement, management, and accountability to every public service.

Once American citizens know what to expect in the performance and management of public schools and services, results will be greatly improved, and our future economic success and social progress assured.

CAUTIONS

These measures are not perfect. They only measure basic skills. Many things educators try to do are not measurable; there is little point in trying. But some things are important, and they should be measured. You cannot measure everything: poetry, philosophy, music, art, creativity, thinking, existential literature; for instance. Do not even bother to try.

You cannot do it all yourself. You will need your school board's cooperation. If you are a parent checking out a new community, ask the superintendent or principal if the district surveys parents and analyzes test scores. If not, try another community. If so, ask to see the results. If you are already settled and your board is not doing this, suggest that they do. Give them this book so they will know it can be done. If you are a taxpayer wondering whether you are getting your money's worth from your taxes, follow the same procedures.

Later in this book you will see actual results from districts in a variety of communities, and some especially heartening improvement stories of successful districts in urban areas.

12

Management: Positive Support for Teachers and Administrators

Policies and practices of school governance, management, and performance have a significant impact on results. How people are treated makes a big difference in their performance. Key management requirements are the following:

- Board policies to encourage teamwork and accountability
- Participative management to provide positive support for staff
- Performance measures to focus on purpose and measure results.

These lessons of the behavioral sciences and applied psychology have their roots in the Renaissance, humanism, the Enlightenment and scientific method. They helped fuel America's national democracy and its industrial and agricultural revolutions. They are needed in the management of schools and public services, too.

Communication, teamwork, trust, and confidence should replace conflict.

- Unions have been a positive influence in raising teacher salaries, improving working conditions, and getting rid of traditional authoritarian administration. They should also seek effective management, to produce good performance and justify salaries and budgets, rather than just adversarial relationships.
- School boards should encourage teamwork and accountability, through policies and behavior, avoiding both overinvolvement and "rubber stamp" extremes.

Positive management is needed with planning, organization, information, evaluation, development, and compensation for teachers and administrators. Performance-based administrative compensation is often the first step.

Participative management has become axiomatic in almost every successful American business, especially in consumer products and services. Consumer goods industries have long known that a marketing orientation is essential, and that the careful nurturing of staff talent is a necessity. America's pharmaceutical research labs, advertising agencies, law firms, consulting firms, accounting firms, architectural firms— all have been successful by being well managed. Common factors are an emphasis on good performance, responsiveness to consumers, high standards of quality, aggressive recruitment to get the talent that is needed, and positive, supportive management of these people once they are in the organization, with positive staff relationships to encourage, recognize, and reward good performance.

It is these techniques that must be applied to America's schools and public services.

THE SCHOOL MANAGEMENT MODEL

My 15 years of research and experience with hundreds of schools and districts across the country have led to a complete system of participative management with performance measures and board accountability that is

Participative with positive support and relationships of communication, teamwork, trust, and confidence

Accountable to the public with objective performance information as well as teamwork and communication.

This is a system to extend the public management revolution of participatory democracy and scientific method to schools (as America previously replaced authority with freedom in national government, and showed the world how to improve productivity in agriculture and industry).

The system is implemented through a participative and accountable management process that includes the following:

- *Organization* clearly defined, with documented responsibilities and relationships
- *Planning* that starts with a realistic assessment of the situation in each school and department
- *Information* documenting performance

—Student learning and development, parent satisfaction and public confidence, teacher morale and job satisfaction, cost-effectiveness

—Surveys of parents and teachers; analysis of test scores (growth rates, achievement/ability, patterns)

—Outside audit to ensure accuracy and credibility

· *Evaluation* that is fair and effective

—Administrative evaluation based on performance, responsibilities and goals, information and development

—Teacher evaluation that is positive and participative, accepted and supported by staff

· *Administrative compensation* with categories, targets, and ranges based on responsibilities and outside comparisons

· *Board policies* and superintendent leadership for teamwork and accountability.

These steps lead to more learning and cost-effectiveness; justify budgets and salaries; improved confidence, morale, teamwork, and accountability; assure a sound foundation for board decision making; and demonstrate that taxpayers are getting their money's worth.

Participative management starts by asking people—teachers, parents, and students—what they think. Get a realistic picture of the situation in each district, school, and classroom through discussion and perceptions. Develop a vision of strengths and improvement opportunities, a sense of direction for the future. Then get some solid data indicating multiple views of performance focused on mission and purpose. Keep in mind the benefits of hard, factual data like what resulted from applying the scientific method to America's farms. Remember the benefits of considering customer and staff perceptions that resulted from application of the behavioral sciences to business. Use these data to identify improvement opportunities, to prove where a good job is being done, to get the board to be positive with policies of teamwork and accountability instead of conflict and fragmentation, to convince taxpayers they are getting their money's worth, and to get the funding needed for good schools and fair salaries.

Management should provide a connection between your board and staff. In Chicago and many other American big cities, schools have operated for years without any connection between the central office and the staff except for bureaucratic red tape and passing the buck. Many smaller districts, too, have evaluation systems that exist only on paper.

Assessing the management of your district will be more difficult than either governance or performance; but you can do it. Here are the criteria we use:

· Administrative and teacher responsibility for performance should be nailed down in a clear-cut, definitive organization chart and position descriptions emphasizing responsibility for performance in student learning, public confidence, parent satisfaction, teacher morale, and overall cost-effectiveness.

- Your district should be responsive to the needs and desires of parents, students, teachers, and other staff members.

- Look for staff relationships of participation, communication, teamwork, trust, and confidence—not the conflict and fragmentation that have too often characterized schools in the past.

- Make sure your district has a planning process with goals and objectives based on a realistic assessment of the situation in each school and department. The planning process should involve a team including central office administrators, principals, and department heads.

- Information—such as test data analysis to indicate student learning and parent/teacher surveys to indicate their satisfaction and concerns noted above—should be used to improve performance, build confidence, and provide positive reinforcement.

- Administrative evaluation and compensation should be based on performance, using the kind of information noted above, with plenty of room for judgment, and emphasis on development. Look for a plan like those common in industry, with categories, targets, and ranges based on market comparisons with plenty of room inside the range to reward good performance.

- Insist upon teacher evaluation that is fair, effective, and operational. This is often the weakest link in school management—not fully effective in more than 10 percent of the districts I have observed.

- Be sure your district is aggressive in recruitment, selection, and development of staff. Education is a people business, and will be successful only if we get our fair share of the nation's talent; recruit aggressively, select carefully, and develop effectively.

Part VI of this book presents the details of a positive system of organization, evaluation, and compensation to assure the competence needed on the part of both administrators and teachers to get the job done. Performance-based compensation is the key to an effective, practical system that replaces conflict with teamwork and decline with success.

ACCOUNTABILITY SYSTEM/PARTICIPATIVE MANAGEMENT

The system for board accountability through participative management is summarized in Exhibit 9. The four key factors that link the organization with accountability are planning, information, evaluation, and compensation. In effect, the board is offering fairness and support in exchange for measures of results and performance-based compensation. Consequently, there is more productivity and job satisfaction for staff—an upward spiral of teamwork and success, instead of conflict and decline.

Planning

Planning has three key parts:

Document responsibilities with an emphasis on performance and leadership. An overall concept of how the organization is expected to work and insistence upon responsibility for performance are most important. Accurate, up-to-date job descriptions for administrators and teachers are also needed.

Establish goals. As part of the planning process, goals should be set for the district, school, and each administrator and teacher—a management-by-objective process.

Analyze performance and improvement opportunities in each school, department, and classroom. The situation in each school, department, and classroom should be analyzed by each responsible administrator and, if possible, by each teacher, either with the immediate supervisor or, where possible, with a committee. Often this analysis is better conducted orally, since written reports require a great deal of time and effort to produce. Moreover, issues difficult to write about can often be discussed readily, such as the character of a community with problems such as poverty and mobility, or the circumstances of a high school department where some teachers may be experiencing personal problems and relationships may be strained.

Information

The outside audit provides objective documentation of performance and interpretation of results in the context of patterns and trends in other districts. The focus is on test data analysis to measure learning and parent/teacher surveys to measure satisfaction.

Evaluation

Administrative evaluation is based on planning and performance information. Without these two factors, there is no real administrative responsibility for performance. With planning and performance information, administrative evaluation can be based on achievements compared with objectives, and on objective information about student learning and parent/teacher satisfaction. The outside audit helps to ensure fairness and accuracy.

Exhibit 9
Participative Management: Positive Support for Teachers and Administrators

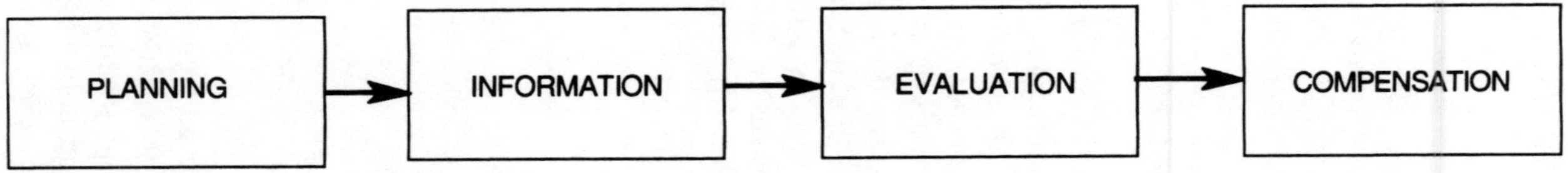

```
┌──────────┐     ┌─────────────┐     ┌────────────┐     ┌──────────────┐
│ PLANNING │ ──▶ │ INFORMATION │ ──▶ │ EVALUATION │ ──▶ │ COMPENSATION │
└──────────┘     └─────────────┘     └────────────┘     └──────────────┘
```

Responsibilities

Goals

Situation Analysis

Student Learning
Test Data Analysis

Parent/Teacher
Satisfaction
Surveys

Job Performance
Planning/Results
Audit Information
Personal
Development

Categories, Ranges
Internal Equity
Outside Comparisons
Policies

Other requirements of effective schools, to support this administrative accountability system:

· Operational, fair, effective teacher evaluation
· Communication, participation, trust, and confidence
· Board policies and behavior supporting teamwork and accountability.

In effect, the board is offering fairness and support in exchange for information
and performance-based compensation.

Compensation

Evaluation provides the basis for performance-based administrative compensation. Plans for school districts look much like those for management in industry: categories, ranges, and targets; analysis of internal and external equity; comparing salaries for jobs with similar responsibilities internally and with similar organizations externally.

Insistence on a fair and effective system for evaluating teachers and administrators is central to the fulfillment of responsibility for performance. Everyone who has ever been involved in a personal service knows that quality must be monitored. Teachers, like doctors, lawyers, research scientists, advertising executives, and service personnel everywhere, know that not everyone can do a good job, and not everyone continues to do a good job. My experience is that about 1 percent of good teaching faculty fail annually. This may seem a small number, but if it is allowed to accumulate over 20 or 30 years—remember that most urban and many other school systems in America have no evaluation at present—you can see how the impact on performance could be dramatic.

Do not think of evaluation as negative. It should be used to support performance improvements and personal development. Recruitment and selection of teachers and administrators to suit the requirements of specific schools is essential. Part of the problem in many urban communities is that teachers who chose to teach in middle-class ethnic communities have seen those communities change to working-class black. This is a difficult problem, exacerbated by the computerized selection process in many big city school districts that virtually precludes personal judgment about the motivation and capacity of the teacher to teach in a particular school and to work with a particular kind of student. An upscale suburb with demanding parents is simply a different kind of challenge that takes a different kind of teacher—not better or worse—than does working with blacks in the central city or Latinos who do not speak English.

Fair, effective teacher evaluation is especially important, and difficult. Characteristics we have found common to successful plans are shown in Chapter 22.

TEACHER MERIT PAY

Do not try to start with merit pay for teachers. Communication, evaluation, and information are prerequisites. But do base total board budget decisions, and administrative compensation, on performance. The best place to begin, in most districts, is with an outside audit of performance information—analysis of test scores for student learning, and parent/teacher surveys to measure their satisfaction and identify concerns. This will give you a baseline for improvement, contribute one essential ingredient of board accountability, confidence, and support, and provide the basis of objective information on which you can build fair compensation, recognition, and reward.

Then turn to strengthening your internal management systems, beginning with administrators. At the same time, begin to reach out to teachers with more participation and communication, and finally address the difficult issue of a fair and effective evaluation and development plan for teachers, which you undoubtedly will have to do with their participation, and in an atmosphere of trust and confidence.

For specific examples of organization, evaluation, and compensation plans, see Part VI of this book. There you will find successful examples for setting salaries and evaluating administrators, and a positive, participative approach to teacher evaluation based on interviews to find out what teachers want and need.

13

Governance: Democracy, Teamwork, and Success

American school boards today have an extraordinary opportunity to strengthen local democracy, almost as great as our country's founding fathers, and equal to the political leaders, academics, businessmen, and farmers who gave us the industrial and agricultural revolutions that made America the world leader of the twentieth century. The public management revolution will be just as important to America's progress and success in the twenty-first century. As our country enters a new era of reform, beginning in schools, boards are under increasing pressure: to prove that a good job is being done; to build productive staff relations of teamwork and accountability; to strengthen performance and management. This chapter and Part VII focus on these key board responsibilities.

The public management revolution beginning in schools is one of America's most important and exciting public issues—now, and for many years to come. School board members, with district staff—as well as citizens, taxpayers, parents, and students—all have vitally important roles to play if American education is to have the quality we must have to meet our needs. Although school board members are in some respects the least important part of the district team—compared, for instance, with full-time staff members—in other ways they have the most powerful impact on performance. This chapter speaks directly of their critically important responsibilities, and also provides a framework for the community to evaluate elected representatives and the job they are doing on our behalf. American school boards are no longer tolerant of their traditional role of being merely rubber stamps for the superintendent's authority. They are insisting on information and a positive role in decision making. Sometimes they may go too far, meddling in administrative responsibilities and raising the rate of superintendent turnover beyond what is fair and reasonable.

In addition to a general policy supported by board behavior encouraging teamwork, responsiveness, and participation as well as performance and results, every school board ought to do two specific things to be sure it is accountable:

• One is an outside audit of key performance indicators, such as test scores and parent/teacher surveys. This is the same kind of objective performance information as a basis for accountability that an industrial board of directors receives in an audited financial report. Remember, in schools performance is not primarily financial. If you are going to base compensation, budgets, and other decisions on performance, you must be sure you have comparable, credible information.

• Second, every school board should receive superintendent reports of the evaluation process and results for programs, administrators, and teachers. Traditional secrecy in this regard cannot be tolerated by boards who wish to be accountable.

A SYSTEM OF ACCOUNTABILITY AND TEAMWORK

School boards need policies of accountability and improvement instead of secrecy and decline, and policies of teamwork and delegation instead of conflict and authority, as shown in Exhibit 10.

Accountability

Measuring performance justifies participative management and delegation, teamwork and support, needed funding and fair salaries. Unlike some traditional curriculum approaches, with overly detailed control, this is based on key indicators and an outside audit. The two sides of the system are used to justify and to make each other possible— performance measures and participative management. The board is neither a rubber stamp nor overinvolved, teachers are fully represented and participating, and responsibility for performance is shared by board and staff.

Teamwork

Positive support for teachers and administrators is provided through fair and effective organization, planning, information, evaluation, and compensation. Communication, participation, and responsiveness are key factors. Delegation and positive support are justified by key indi-

Exhibit 10
Teamwork and Accountability

This is a system of participative and results-oriented management for team-work and accountability.

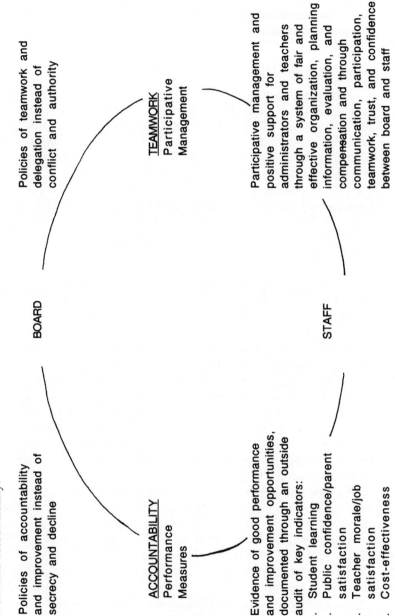

Policies of teamwork and delegation instead of conflict and authority

BOARD

TEAMWORK
Participative Management

Participative management and positive support for administrators and teachers through a system of fair and effective organization, planning information, evaluation, and compensation and through communication, participation, teamwork, trust, and confidence between board and staff

STAFF

Policies of accountability and improvement instead of secrecy and decline

ACCOUNTABILITY
Performance Measures

Evidence of good performance and improvement opportunities, documented through an outside audit of key indicators:
. Student learning
. Public confidence/parent satisfaction
. Teacher morale/job satisfaction
. Cost-effectiveness

cators of performance. This side of the equation owes much to the behavioral sciences, through the child study movement and other humanistic influences. Performance measures are used positively to justify delegation and salaries, to build confidence and morale, to improve learning and cost-effectiveness.

RESPONSIBILITIES OF DIRECTORS

School boards are not the only governing directors to come under increasing pressure to demonstrate their responsibility. Many business boards have discovered their liability and the need for careful defining and balancing of the interests to which they are responsible in an era of corporate takeovers. Hospital boards are under increasing pressure to demonstrate good performance. All of these groups stand at the fulcrum of leverage to be sure that society and the public interest are being well served by the organizations that serve us. These bodies exercise oversight of the connection between the institution and society. Many businesses now see this responsibility as multiple: involving the community, owners, customers, and employees; this model applies reasonably to schools as well.

The concept of local governing boards goes back to the very roots of civilization. You can trace the history of American local government through its English predecessors and in turn its Germanic roots, for instance, through words like "alderman." Or you can find starting points in Eastern Europe, Greece, Rome, the city-states, the Hanseatic League, American Indians. Almost every culture has some form of governance centered on local communities. The ideas that organizations serve the people, that how well they do so is the responsibility of their boards, and that this should be measured are relatively new concepts. Certainly they contrast sharply with the authoritarian history of organizations designed to serve the interests of the robber barons, or in earlier eras the landed gentry or nobility, with workers seen merely as tools or even as slaves.

Modern management with its concepts of customer satisfaction, product quality, job satisfaction, and participation for staff, and organizations that are ultimately measured by their contribution to society, are relatively new ideas but they are favored by the trends of history, away from authority and toward participation, independence, freedom, and democracy. School board members should understand the critically important role they play, and the personal contribution they can make to moving forward this process in America.

SCHOOL BOARD CONTRIBUTIONS TO THE PUBLIC MANAGEMENT REVOLUTION

School board responsibilities are particularly exciting today because of the public management revolution beginning in schools. Adding a third level to the traditional American dichotomy between board policies and administrative responsibilities—measuring performance—will have a tremendous positive impact on America's future public service productivity and effectiveness. Services in the next century will be the dominant part of our society. Many of these services will be public (although the distinction may become increasingly blurred, as we realize that all organizations are intended to serve the public interest). Therefore, the opportunity for positive impact by school board members is particularly great.

I know from personal experience that most board members perceive their service as motivated by a desire to give something back to their local community, often during the time their own children are in school. Naturally this local contribution is an important part of their duties. But it is also important for every school board member to conceive of his or her contribution to the broader progress of America's development of management and improvement of performance in public services. The steps outlined in this book for strengthening performance, management, and governance are for this purpose. School board members may perceive their objectives in narrow terms, such as controlling costs on behalf of taxpayers, improving reading and writing skills, accelerating foreign language study, or any of hundreds of other specific objectives that are worthwhile and important in their own right. My focus in this book is broader.

Local democracy is the oldest and finest form of public service, and school boards are America's best expression of this tradition. American school boards can have a powerful, positive impact on district management and performance through policies of teamwork and accountability. To do so, they must select, guide, and evaluate the superintendent with this in mind. School board leverage for improvement comes to a focus in evaluating the superintendent, and this interface has not been without its problems in recent years. As administrative authority has been eroded by teacher unions demanding participation and fairness on the one hand, and school boards demanding greater involvement in decision making on the other, pressures on the superintendent and other administrators have intensified. The survival rate of superintendents has declined to an average of as little as two or three years.

American school boards are one of the world's leading examples of effective democracy. Both board policies and superintendent leadership are important. The focus should be on teamwork and accountability, people and results, performance and management. Reform pressures are strong on local school boards today—to make sure that a good job is being done, and to prove it. Obviously this is the most important level of action for real reform.

The school board's role in this process is small but critically important. The philosophy, attitude, and behavior of the board will affect the entire performance of the district, determining whether it is a well-managed, high-performing district or one that is pulling down the national average. To meet their responsibilities successfully, boards should concentrate on these four key elements:

- Build teamwork—develop and implement a policy of communication, participation, teamwork, trust, and confidence.
- Measure results—develop, analyze, and use performance information to show where a good job is being done and to identify improvement opportunities.
- Insist on accountability—using the planning, information, evaluation, and compensation system described in this book.
- Evaluate staff—using techniques that are fair and effective for teachers and administrators to support positive development and improvement.

Finally, boards should use the governance-management-performance system described in this book as the framework for selecting and evaluating a superintendent, whose leadership is critically important in successfully implementing the concept.

Build Teamwork

Develop and implement a policy of communication, participation, teamwork, trust, and confidence. While this is at odds with the prevailing adversarial relationships in schools today, it is the most essential ingredient of good performance, one that often falls directly on the board to initiate.

Communication may need to start with the board, superintendent, and management team. But ultimately the most important groups are the public and the staff. Staff should have ample opportunity for upward communication and for participation in district decision making. For example, a highly visible superintendent, talking personally with each teacher, is a good sign, although naturally it is time consuming. Asking staff to serve on various committees will also provide opportunities for them to communicate concerns and interests. Parent communication and participation are also needed. The most practical tools for stimulating and encouraging communication are surveys of parents and teachers.

Teamwork, trust, and confidence is a long-term building job in most districts, especially where relationships have been strained by collective bargaining. Work hard at it, and remember that it may take a few years to establish.

Measure Performance

Develop, analyze, and use performance information—to show where a good job is being done and to identify improvement opportunities. The most important function is analysis of student learning using test scores and of parent/teacher satisfaction using surveys. Your reaction when your own child brings home a report card obviously varies if the grades are A or F. Positive reinforcement for an A is just as important as concern and help for the F. But most school board members do not know whether their teachers are getting As or Fs—running a 4-minute mile or a 30-minute mile. Many boards are dissatisfied and unappreciative regardless of actual performance, so teachers get discouraged.

The remedy is performance information. Find out how much your students are learning and how this compares with other districts. Find out what your parents and teachers are satisfied with and what they're concerned about, and again compare this with patterns in other districts. Use this information to build confidence where performance is good, as you would treat your child if he or she brought home an A. Where the evidence of performance is not good, use it to show need for improvement and to focus priorities on those areas.

Standardized achievement tests are a uniquely American and well-developed source of performance information, yet most boards do not know how to use them. One board member described the pattern in his district as starting at the sixtieth percentile in the first grade and winding up at the fortieth percentile by high school. Then he asked if this was a problem. Of course it was a problem! Boards must understand test scores. They must receive a simple, straightforward presentation that helps them to do so. While many states have taken the lead in mandating published test scores and improvement, a local board must understand these data, to make sure that real improvements are occurring.

Complementing the hard data of test scores are attitudes and opinions of parents, teachers, students, and taxpayers. Use surveys to give you a sound basis for understanding satisfactions and concerns. Emphasize the positives. And do something about the negatives.

If every school board would take these three simple steps of analyzing test scores and surveying parents and teachers, a substantial improvement in performance could be achieved.

Evaluate Staff

Establish evaluation systems that are fair and effective for teachers and administrators. First you must be sure your administrators are evaluated on the basis of progress against objectives and their job description. Use the performance information described above as a framework for reasonable standards and expectations. Be sure the process is individualized and that the superintendent spends time communicating with administrators about performance. Do not hesitate to tie administrative performance to compensation. The mechanics for doing so are fully proven in schools.

Equally important to an effective school is teacher evaluation. But the process is challenging. Many districts will need to wait until trust and confidence are sufficiently established, so that delicate issues can be addressed. Begin by asking teachers their attitudes and concerns about evaluation. You will find that they want to be evaluated, and that many evaluation practices used in the past were neither fair nor effective.

Insist on Accountability

Use performance information, teamwork and administrative responsibility, to support teacher effectiveness. Administrative responsibility, evaluation, and compensation are the fulcrum leveraging board accountability up and teacher effectiveness down. Teamwork and accountability are supported by communication and a feedback system regarding student learning, and parent and teacher satisfaction, from the bottom of the organization to the top. An industrial board of directors has this in the form of audited financial statements and sales data. In a school, the outside audit fulfills this function.

From a teacher's point of view, this support system makes the job more satisfying and productive. Teacher effectiveness is supported by a system of selection and recruitment, evaluation and development, communication and participation, that is responsive to teacher needs for materials, facilities, or training. All of this effort is focused on the purpose and mission of the organization: student learning, parent satisfaction and public confidence, teacher morale and cost-effectiveness.

Part VII deals more narrowly with the focal point of board/superintendent responsibilities:

• How the board can monitor administrative performance through

—Superintendent reporting of the evaluation process
—Objective performance information about learning and parent/teacher satisfaction validated in an outside audit

• Criteria and process for the board to evaluate the superintendent
• District performance and management standards

The board's most useful catalyst to move in the direction of measuring results is an outside audit of performance involving test data analysis of student learning and parent/teacher surveys of satisfaction.

V

Measure Your School to Evaluate and Improve

14

The Outside Audit School Performance Formula: Learning, Confidence, Morale, and Cost-Effectiveness

Schools can be measured. This chapter and the next five show how. Do not put your child in school, do not move to a new community, do not pay your taxes—and if you are a school board member, do not vote to approve budgets and salaries—without applying these tests of good school performance first. Use the tools in this chapter to measure your school and district, to see if you are getting your money's worth.

MEASURE RESULTS

The first step to improving school performance is pragmatic measures for education like those which led to America's achievements in agriculture and industry. The educational counterparts of business measures, such as earnings per share and return on investment, are symbolized in the following formula:

$$\frac{\text{Learning} \times \text{Confidence} \times \text{Morale}}{\text{Cost}}$$

The four components of the formula are the following:

- *Learning*—student learning and development, measured by the analysis of standardized achievement test scores, especially growth rates, and other key indicators (Growth rates are calculated by, for example, subtracting last year's fourth grade score from this year's fifth grade score. You should get a year's growth for a year in school, a simple standard that anyone can apply.)

- *Confidence*—parent satisfaction and public confidence, and perceived improvement opportunities, measured by surveys
- *Morale*—teacher and staff satisfaction, opinions and concerns, also measured by surveys
- *Cost*—expenditures to achieve these results.

Applying this formula in hundreds of schools and districts across the country has shown a wide range of results:

- The worst school was achieving no growth in student learning.
- The best achieved more than two years of growth for a year in school.
- Some low-achieving schools in our central cities have doubled student learning. They are now achieving more than a full year of growth for a year in school, exceeding the performance of many suburbs.

This is the kind of achievement we need in all of America's schools if our country is to be competitive in a world economy, eliminate the underclass, and continue our economic success and social progress into the twenty-first century.

Student learning is not the only improvement. These districts are also raising the satisfaction of teachers and parents, from levels as low as 50 percent in some cases to as high as 100 percent. They are doing this with confidence and morale, teamwork and accountability. And they are not spending more to achieve these improved results.

Of course this formula is not a perfect or complete representation of school performance. It focuses on the basics. As people first seek to meet their needs for food and shelter, and then turn to higher objectives, so the basic skills are building blocks that all students need.

USE INFORMATION

The first step in improving school performance is to measure it. Use this information to prove where a good job is being done, to build public confidence, to provide positive reinforcement for staff, and to identify improvement opportunities. The most vital information is analysis of student learning using test scores, and analysis of parent/teacher satisfaction using surveys. Your reaction when your child brings a report card home varies. Positive reinforcement for an A is just as important as concern and help for an F.

But most school boards do not have a report card to evaluate their teachers. They have no idea whether their schools are running a 4-minute mile or a 30-minute mile. Some boards are dissatisfied and unappreciative, regardless of actual performance. So naturally teachers get discouraged. The good ones do not receive the pat on the back they deserve and need to keep going. The poor ones are not disciplined in any way, let alone dismissed.

The remedy is performance information. Find out how much students are learning and how this compares with other districts. Find out what parents and teachers are satisfied with and what their concerns are, and again compare this with patterns in other districts. Use this information to build confidence where performance is good. Where the performance is not good, use the evidence to show need for improvement and to focus priorities on realistic improvement opportunities.

The board must understand test scores. They must receive a simple, straightforward presentation that helps them to do so. While many states have taken the lead in mandating published test scores and improvements, a local board must understand these data to make sure that real improvements occur. Also, these numbers should be reported to the public in a form that they can understand. Complementing these scores are attitudes and opinions of parents, teachers, students, and taxpayers. Use surveys to understand their satisfaction and concerns. Emphasize the positives, and do something about the negatives.

If every school district would take these simple steps of analyzing test scores and surveying parents and teachers, a substantial improvement in performance could be achieved. I have seen districts double student learning, from 6 months to 12 months of growth per year, and increase parent and teacher satisfaction from 50 percent to 100 percent. There is a surprising difference in performance between districts that are similar in the nature of the community and population served. Some schools are achieving as much as two years' growth for a year in school while others show no growth at all. Taxpayers and parents concerned about getting their money's worth and about making sure their students are well educated must be sure that their school boards, superintendents, administrators, and teachers are aware of these results, and are acting accordingly, rather than merely talking about good performance.

From my 15 years of experience, I would estimate that no more than 10 percent of America's schools and districts meet the criteria in this chapter for the availability, analysis, use, and publication of understandable information about performance that is essential for accountability. It is up to you to make sure your district is on the right side of this proportion.

By multiplying the factors in the formula, I have seen districts with scores as low as 1 and as high as 20. A score of 20 is achieved by a growth rate of 15 months per year times 100 percent parent satisfaction and 100 percent teacher satisfaction divided by a cost factor of 75 percent of the county average. A score of 1 is achieved by a growth rate of 5 months per year times parent satisfaction of 50 percent and teacher satisfaction of 50 percent divided by a cost factor of 125 percent of the county average. This formula is obviously an oversimplified representation of school performance. But the fact that one school or district differs from a similar one by such a dramatic amount is remarkable.

Finally, each district needs to be analyzing test scores on a classroom-by-classroom, teacher-by-teacher, and student-by-student basis as well. The credibility, accuracy, and comparison of these surveys and test data analyses require outside objectivity, credibility, and perspective.

CAUTIONS

Of course there are limitations on performance information. No one single indicator is reliable in its own right. Test data must be viewed for at least five to ten years in order to see patterns and trends. They should be analyzed within the context of a knowledge of patterns in districts of varied types (urban, rural, suburban) and at various socioeconomic levels. Personal impressions and observations should not be put aside in favor of information, but should either be reinforced and confirmed by hard data or corrected so that perceptions of board members, administrators, and teachers are more nearly in line with reality.

It is important not to provide overly strong incentives that encourage teachers to spend too much time on things that are tested and not enough on those that are not, or to manipulate the data in ways that look more favorable. However, with the comprehensive information recommended in this book, such fiddling with data is unlikely; it would have to be done on such a massive scale and over so many years that it would be virtually impossible.

THE VALUE OF INFORMATION

The school performance formula can help parents and teachers, as well as board members and administrators, define the mission and purpose of schools and understand how well they are being achieved.

Cost

Obviously costs are an important factor in school performance. Surprisingly, they do not always vary in proportion to the three output measures. In fact, some high-performance districts are also low expenditure ones. The output factors noted above—student learning, parent satisfaction, and teacher satisfaction—vary more dramatically than costs. One difference between private industry and public schools is the relatively fixed cost of education. Surprisingly, cost is the formula factor with the least variation between districts. In the formula, cost is calculated by comparing the cost per student in your district with the local county average. For example, if your cost is $5,000 and the county average is $4,000, you are at 125 percent. A typical range is 75 percent to 125 percent. This is a much narrower range than we have found for other components of the formula. Often high-spending districts are not high-performing districts. Those which are doing a good job are getting much more for their money than the others.

Of course, controlling costs is important, but do not expect to find substantial improvement opportunities in most districts. The key cost factors are staff/student ratios, salaries, tax rates, and debt policy. (See Chapter 19.) Because of the narrow range of costs and limited opportunities for their reduction in most districts, improvement of performance must concentrate on outputs: student learning and parent/teacher satisfaction. Unlike costs, these factors vary over a surprisingly wide range: student learning ranges from zero to two years' growth for a single year in school. The proportion of satisfied parents also varies over a range as great as two to one.

Learning

The greatest difference in performance between districts, and often the biggest improvement opportunity, is student learning.

Test Data Analysis

Percentiles, grade equivalents, and especially growth rates must be analyzed at district, school, classroom, and student levels, preferably for a period at least as long as five–ten years to provide a clear indication of performance and trends. Then these data need to be considered in the context of experience and patterns in other districts. This helps to reassure taxpayers, parents, and board members by proving where a good job is being done and by identifying possible improvement opportunities. The most difficult aspect of analyzing test data to measure student learning is that test scores vary with a community's income levels and socioeconomic status. The way to get around this problem is to use growth rates—calculated, for example, by subtracting last year's fourth grade score from this year's fifth grade score. On this basis, every district can and should achieve a full year's growth (ten months) for a year in school. I have seen districts realizing as little as half a year's growth for a year in school, and as much as a year and a half.

The second level of analysis is to look for this growth rate—a year for a year in school—in each subject, grade, and school. Here the range of actual performance is even wider, ranging from zero to two full years.

Growth Rates

The single most important measure of student learning is average annual growth. Test scores rise as you move up the socioeconomic ladder, varying with the student's family background and support at home. Growth rates, however, reveal what good management and effective teaching can produce. Poor communities with minority students can achieve growth rates as high as upscale suburbs, a nice leveling feature of this particular measurement. By accumulating these growth rates over the years, you can see what a startling difference there can be between two neighboring districts, or between two schools in the same district. At one extreme, with a growth rate of only half a year per year in school, only 4 years' worth of learning is achieved during 8 years in school. On the other hand, growing a year and a half per year in school packs 12 years' worth of learning into 8 years of school.

Some high-growth districts are low-cost districts. They could be achieving three times as much and investing less, a remarkable difference in return on investment. Teachers are generally comfortable with this concept of value added because that is the way they deal with individual children. There is a tradition in American schools, especially at the elementary level, often expressed as "We take each child where he is and move him as far as we can." The concept of growth rates and value added fits this much better than test scores. And value added is more a measure of teacher contribution and less of the parents' income, family support at home, or the child's intelligence.

Teachers' Importance

Learning improvements being achieved in urban, suburban, and rural communities prove that teachers really do make a difference, especially where students do not have many advantages when they begin school. This is only common sense, but it runs counter to what some academic researchers have observed by correlating test scores with the socioeconomic character of communities. This seems to indicate that the education, wealth, status, and success of parents are the primary determinants of student learning. This simply is not true. Growth rates are the real measure of student learning, and by this measure the teacher is indeed a major factor.

Other Indicators

In addition to growth rates, it is important to look at percentiles of achievement and to compare these with ability. However, many districts that have been able to raise the percentiles of achievement have found ability scores following along, indicating that students' IQ scores were not being fully and fairly revealed by tests that depend on language skills. It is also important to look at grade equivalent scores and trends, though this is the least useful indicator. We use it mainly to calulate growth rates. In high schools, additional tests are available; but they are not as comprehensive in their coverage of learning objectives at this level. SAT and ACT scores are relevant. Various contests and competitions should be considered (see Chapter 18).

Other indicators have been successfully utilized by high school department heads in measuring their own performance. To illustrate, I have seen surveys of graduates confirming that many students wind up in jobs to which their home economics courses, for instance, were directly related. Some high school physical education departments do a very fine job of measuring students' performance against national standards of physical capability, such as the number of push-ups, chin-ups, and sit-ups they can do. Attendance, drop-out, and discipline statistics are also relevant and should be analyzed.

CONFIDENCE

The second key output factor is "customer" satisfaction. This is best measured by a written survey of parents, delivered to every parent at home, and tabulated by an outside service. The sample survey in Chapter 15 indicates the practical, straightforward questions that are needed. Surveys add subjectivity to the hard data of test scores. Naturally, parents are not always right, but their perceptions are always relevant. Surveys are a helpful tool, showing you in what areas parents are satisfied and, more important, in what areas they are not. Satisfaction reinforces good work by staff; identified concerns become next year's priorities.

Students, graduates, and taxpayers can also be surveyed. The latter tend to have little information on schools, with opinions difficult to act upon. Nevertheless, in most districts taxpayers who are not parents with children currently in school represent more than 80 percent of residents; obviously their opinions must be considered. Students and graduates provide an excellent source of information, especially at upper grade levels. By college they are virtually the only source, and an extremely valuable one, although often best tapped informally rather than through surveys. I have worked with universities and graduate schools that have made excellent use of feedback from both written surveys and personal discussions with students, and I have seen this used very effectively in high schools and among graduates of elementary schools. Even first graders can circle happy and sad faces, indicating their perceptions of their teacher in a useful way.

In many districts parent satisfaction is very high. But a handful of concerns can be identified that become action points for planning. These might be dissatisfaction with the science curriculum, use of computers, bus stop locations, lunch quality, building cleanliness, responsiveness of principals and teachers to parent concerns, or any one of the other items in the survey. This is extremely useful information because instead of spreading efforts over a wide range of items, many of which may be completely satisfactory, the focus can be on those which are matters of real concern. Often the opinions of a large group of parents are different from those of a few activists who may be pestering the school board about specific concerns that are not widely shared.

MORALE

The third output factor is teacher satisfaction. This provides a nice balance to the parent survey; questions can be virtually identical. Typically there is a great deal of similarity between the opinions of parents, teachers, and students as to both strengths and weaknesses of a district's performance. By triangulating these three sources of opinions, if a problem is identified by all three, you can be reasonably confident that it is at least worth looking into. In addition to the questions that parallel the parent survey, the teacher survey in Chapter 16 has a section dealing with working conditions, evaluation, communication, and internal relationships. These are important issues today. Unions provide teachers with a vehicle for complaining, but not necessarily for remedying deficiencies in these areas. The survey is a more direct communication device and tends to encourage action and response. No one source of information by itself would be adequate to evaluate a school district. But when you put these three components together, you have a good basis either for confidence and improvement opportunities or, if there are serious problems, for more extensive action.

Surveys offer two other important advantages. They put the entire organization on notice that parents are to be responded to in a way that generally keeps them satisfied. This is not easy in education, and it is not quite fair to say that the customer is always right. Sometimes parents are not correct in what they want for their children, but a district that tries to respond to parents in this way will be able to satisfy most of them. The same is true of teachers. Rather than having an adversarial relationship with administrators, a teacher survey by itself demonstrates that administrators must be responsive to the needs and desires of teachers. Obviously this cannot extend to every book or piece of equipment that a teacher might want, but it must at least cover the basics in order to keep teachers satisfied. The survey reinforces the need for the organization to be responsive to its staff, and this is valuable even apart from the performance information it provides.

Specific and detailed examples of each of these measures—confidence, morale, learning, and costs—are shown in the next few chapters.

15

Parent Survey: How to Improve Parent Satisfaction and Public Confidence

Responsiveness to the customer is one of the most important and valuable innovations of management in business. It is equally applicable, and perhaps even more important, in public services. The simple, straightforward questionnaire for parents at the end of this chapter is one of the most effective steps any school district can take to improve performance. It reassures board, staff, and community where performance is good. It identifies realistic improvement opportunities. An upward spiral of improvement is initiated that will continue until a high plateau is reached and permanently sustained.

Parent survey results provide the same kind of valuable information that a business receives from analyzing sales, profits, and market research. Sales indicate that customers are buying the product. Profitability indicates that the company is able to produce it at a cost less than what customers are willing to pay. Market research shows where customers are satisfied, and where improvement opportunities exist. It reveals what may be a different meaning for the customer in the product than what is assumed by those who produce it. Crisco, for example, means one thing to the factory that produces it and quite another to the person using it to bake a cake.

This kind of information is just as important in public services as it is in a business. To understand what the customers want, where they are satisfied, and where they perceive opportunities for improvement is essential to board and staff accountability and good performance. This is perhaps the single most important concept that could be taken from business management and applied to public services. A wonderful contribution could be made to the purposefulness and effectiveness of public services if someone would just ask the customers what they want, where they are satisfied, and where things can be improved.

QUESTIONS

To apply this management technique in schools, we have developed a questionnaire that differs significantly from others you may have seen. From 15 years of research and experience, and interviews with thousands of parents, teachers, students, administrators, and board members, we have developed clear-cut, straightforward questions about performance as they perceive it. These questions do not ask parents to speculate about the future, or philosophize about what might be, but to comment specifically on how their children are doing in school this year, with respect to each category of the academic program and supporting services. Questions are so clear-cut that parents with problems can easily express them. Questions that might have been ruled out by an internal committee because the answers could embarrass someone are included. Do not be afraid of such a hard-hitting survey. This is the only way to build confidence and identify improvement opportunities.

Most schools get very high scores in the view of parents. Those which do not are those which most need to find out where problems are perceived. Of course, as a parent, teacher, taxpayer, or concerned citizen, you do not have to conduct the survey yourself. Expect your school board to use surveys as one way to hold district administrators and staff accountable. If your board is not already using a survey like this one, give them this book to show them why and how they should. And if your school board members still do not understand the value of such a survey, elect some who do.

PROCEDURES

A survey is simple to administer. My experience is that it is best to mail it to every parent in the district. Alternatively, you might try having it filled out at a Parents' Night, but this tends to build some positive bias into results because parents are generally satisfied on these occasions, with a good feeling about the school. And of course you will miss those who do not attend. You also could send it home with students, but this is somewhat uncertain. Some districts have tried to sample parents instead of sending the survey to everyone, but this has two significant disadvantages. One, those parents who are not asked tend to be offended. Two, results will mean more to the administrators and teachers who have to take them seriously if every parent has been asked, even though statistically sample results may be nearly as accurate. Response rates in surveys I have conducted range from 10 percent to 80 percent. The lower level is adequate for useful analysis.

Surveys can be made at any time of the year: spring has a natural logic as the time at which parents can comment on specific school year toward its end. Response rates tend to fall off during the summer, when most people are not thinking as much about schools. And surveys done in the fall may be a little confusing as to whether parents are commenting on this year or last year. However, I have seen surveys successfully conducted at every time of year. The results are so valuable that you may not want to wait until the best time in order to have this essential performance information. A written survey is, in our experience, the most appropriate. Telephoning can be used, but it is generally more expensive and suffers the serious disadvantage that parents cannot know for certain who is on the other end of the line. They may be reluctant to tell a stranger problems that their children are having in school. They may assume the person on the other end of the line is associated with the district, and might feel vindictive toward a child whose parents are not satisfied. These may seem like farfetched possibilities, but experienced survey researchers report that these feelings are common on the part of respondents unless anonymity is assured. Also, written surveys are relatively inexpensive, so you can afford to ask all parents, rather than just a sample: this is more satisfying to parents and more convincing to staff.

If you were a company building a factory on the basis of response to market research, you undoubtedly would want to be much more accurate than the relatively primitive indications given by this survey. However, in our experience this survey is more than adequate for the purpose involved here. The cost side of cost-effectiveness argues for a relatively simple approach. And this has the added advantage of being easily understood by those who must take action: administrators and teachers.

INTERPRETING RESULTS

The answer scale on the questionnaire attached has been simplified to provide only four columns, one of which is "Don't Know." While you could easily think up one or two more columns, we find that these are ample, giving a clear indication where parents are dissatisfied, if that is the case. Interpreting results is remarkably easy. Simply glance down the columns to identify those categories in which you have a large number of "No" responses. These are potential improvement opportunities.

For districts with more than one school, compare results among schools to pinpoint improvement opportunities. In some districts a whole school may be viewed unsatisfactorily by parents; in this case the improvement opportunity is obvious. Remember in interpreting results that parents are not necessarily right. They may misunderstand a program or problem, and schools are naturally somewhat controversial. For one thing, they serve everybody in the community. Parents are sometimes unreasonable in their expectations for their children, or wrong in what they want from the school. Good schools do not necessarily give every single parent what he or she wants; teachers or principals may disagree and argue with parents as to what is best for the child.

OTHER SOURCES

Parents are not the only source of feedback information you should consider. The second most important and useful group of constituents for survey purposes are teachers, a subject covered in detail in Chapter 16. Other staff members may also have useful perceptions and suggestions; with slight modifications this survey can be used for them, too. You should also know what your community thinks of its schools, but this group is not as useful to survey as parents and teachers. For one thing, they will have trouble responding to the detail in this questionnaire; most will not be able to or want to. Second, their opinions on schools will undoubtedly be driven mainly by the opinions of parents who have children in school, so this is a secondary audience in a sense. They may simply be reporting what they read in local newspapers or national magazines rather than what is really going on in your schools. We often give community members a much simpler survey, with the opportunity to request the detail if they wish. Many districts also find personal discussions with constituents very effective.

Obviously a very important group of consumers is students. As they move through the grades, students' opinions will become more valuable and parents' opinions less so, as the students become more astute in assessing their own educational program and as parents become somewhat less familiar with the experiences their children are having in school. Schools should regularly use surveys of students to identify problems and perceptions. Extremely useful surveys of graduates have been conducted by many districts. In both cases, individual and group discussions can be very relevant and helpful.

PERFORMANCE IMPROVEMENTS

Districts using parent surveys have been able to achieve substantial performance improvements. I have personally seen levels of satisfaction with individual schools as low as 50 percent and as high as 100 percent. This gives you an idea of the range of improvement that is possible. After several years of surveys, usually repeated every three or four years, a district will probably find itself without many further improvement opportunities, which of course is good. However, you never know when a changing broader trend, such as rising interest in fiber content of school lunches, or a local incident such as street construction by the city conflicting with bus routes, will create a problem that needs to be identified and resolved. The early warning of possible serious issues is extremely valuable in that action can be taken before the problem becomes too serious.

Surveys are a little frightening, even to high-performing districts, because they may identify a problem. But I have never seen a problem identified that was not manageable and solvable. Sometimes teachers and administrators feel that they must achieve straight As. On the contrary, it is important to have feedback on performance from the customer's view, and to be willing to acknowledge that problems might exist, in order to have the benefits of high satisfaction and confidence that can be achieved with the survey, and realistic identification of improvement opportunities. Otherwise there is a tendency for schools to want to work on everything at the same time; if you can identify perceptions of problems, they are usually a good place to begin. Of course, perceptions are sometimes wrong. Problems may be perceived where they do not exist, or opinions may be based on erroneous information. But these are problems that can be dealt with once the perceptions are documented. Obviously, in these cases the corrective action may be to get the right information communicated.

For example, one district had a low appreciation by its community of its cost-effectiveness, yet it had been forced by economic circumstances to cut virtually 25 percent of the budget and staff that year. The important thing was to get this message out to the community, but that could not be known until these perceptions were identified. Perceptions of various groups about the school are often quite similar. I have done surveys in which parents, teachers, and students all agreed on what were the three most serious problems of the district.

Survey results often differ from what one might expect on the basis of criticisms vocalized by the most active group of parents. Often PTA leaders have an agenda that may differ from that of the general public. Or a few active parents may have interests that are opposite to those of the majority, and yet present them as though they were representative. The only way to find this out is with a survey. This is not a criticism of a few people with specific concerns, just a reminder that it is important to know what the majority thinks.

A major benefit of surveys is to offset what may otherwise be an unfavorable impression created for board members by telephone calls from concerned parents. Since people with positive opinions may not call, it is possible for board members to develop negative impressions from the fact that they receive phone calls from people with concerns. They must have reassurance of broader satisfaction, or solid evidence of concerns, in order to fulfill their accountability. A long-term benefit of surveys is that they build not only immediate board impressions of good performance but also a solid, long-term, documented database of good results that can sustain confidence through short-term problems, difficult incidents, or general concerns that may arise from national publicity about school performance problems.

The best way to introduce you to the simplicity and value of a parent survey is to share one with you. A sample concludes this chapter. Questions are simple and straightforward. They follow a commonsense pattern of what parents expect from schools. They do not ask anything that a parent could not reasonably be expected to know. All subject areas are covered, with sections on relationships and on services such as buses and lunchrooms.

Any parent with a concern finds it easy to express on this survey. Interpretation of results is just as easy. Merely by looking down the list of "No" responses you can see which areas parents are concerned about. The board and staff can use these results to build confidence, to focus priorities for improvement during the coming year, and to monitor improvements achieved in a future survey. As a result, one key factor of performance—public confidence and parent satisfaction—is gradually improved.

I. EDUCATIONAL PROGRAM	Definitely	Partially	No	Don't Know
1. In general, I am satisfied with the school my child is attending.	D	P	N	DK
2. My child is making satisfactory academic progress in school this year.	D	P	N	DK
3. My child likes school this year.	D	P	N	DK
4. My child has effective teachers.	D	P	N	DK
5. The district's academic program is meeting my expectations.	D	P	N	DK
6. The school places enough importance on the basic skills of reading and math.	D	P	N	DK

	Definitely	Partially	No	Don't Know

7. The school has high expectations for the academic achievements of all students.   D   P   N   DK

---

8. My child is learning satisfactorily in:

Reading	D	P	N	DK
Writing	D	P	N	DK
Spelling	D	P	N	DK
Grammar and Punctuation	D	P	N	DK
Mathematics	D	P	N	DK
Social Studies	D	P	N	DK
Science	D	P	N	DK
Music	D	P	N	DK
Art	D	P	N	DK
Physical Education	D	P	N	DK

---

9. I am satisfied with the amount of homework my child has.   D   P   N   DK

If you are not satisfied with the amount of homework, please check one of the following:

Too much _____   Too little _____

---

10. School services are meeting my child's needs satisfactorily in the following areas: (Answer only if your child is currently receiving services.)

Special Education	D	P	N	DK
Psychological Services	D	P	N	DK
Speech Services	D	P	N	DK
Social Work Services	D	P	N	DK
Guidance and Counseling	D	P	N	DK
Gifted Education	D	P	N	DK
Chapter I Reading	D	P	N	DK
Bilingual Program	D	P	N	DK

	Definitely	Partially	No	Don't Know
Nursing	D	P	N	DK
Library/Media	D	P	N	DK

11. The schools' athletic programs are   D   P   N   DK
    appropriate.

12. The schools' extracurricular activities
    are appropriate.   D   P   N   DK

13. The district computer program:

Is worthwhile.	D	P	N	DK
Should be expanded.	D	P	N	DK

14. What changes in the Educational Program would you suggest,
    if any?

    _____

    _____

    _____

	Definitely	Partially	No	Don't Know
II. SCHOOL/COMMUNITY RELATIONS				

1. Cooperation is satisfactory between parents and:

Teachers	D	P	N	DK
Principals	D	P	N	DK
Other District Personnel	D	P	N	DK

2. Teachers know my child well.   D   P   N   DK

3. My children are treated fairly
   in school.   D   P   N   DK

4. I am treated well when I visit
   the school.   D   P   N   DK

5. Student behavior in school is
   satisfactory.   D   P   N   DK

	Definitely	Partially	No	Don't Know
6. School disciplinary practices are appropriate.	D	P	N	DK
7. The report card used is helpful in communicating my child's progress.	D	P	N	DK
8. Parent/teacher conferences are meaningful.	D	P	N	DK
9. Communication is satisfactory between school and parents.	D	P	N	DK
10. Teachers are sufficiently available to meet with parents.	D	P	N	DK

11. How might school/community relations be improved?

_____

_____

_____

III. OTHER SERVICES

	Definitely	Partially	No	Don't Know
1. The Board and Superintendent are fulfilling their responsibilities satisfactorily:				
Board	D	P	N	DK
Superintendent	D	P	N	DK
2. The school district is effectively managed.	D	P	N	DK
3. The school district spends tax dollars wisely.	D	P	N	DK
4. Student bus services are satisfactory.	D	P	N	DK
5. The quality of food served in the hot lunch program is satisfactory.	D	P	N	DK

	Definitely	Partially	No	Don't Know
6. School lunches are priced fairly.	D	P	N	DK
7. Office and secretarial services in the schools are satisfactory.	D	P	N	DK
8. The district's present school buildings are satisfactory in size, location and facilities.	D	P	N	DK
9. The attendance boundaries for schools are satisfactory.	D	P	N	DK
10. School buildings are clean and adequately maintained.	D	P	N	DK
11. The schools have all the books, materials, supplies and equipment needed for educational and other purposes.	D	P	N	DK

12. What changes would you suggest, if any?

_____

_____

_____

16

Teacher Survey: How to Improve Teacher Morale and Job Satisfaction

Participation of staff in decision making and in communicating problems and concerns is one of the most important areas of progress in modern management. It parallels the gradual shift from authoritarianism to participative democracy in government and political affairs and a generally greater freedom of choice open to individuals in the modern world.

The teacher survey at the end of this chapter parallels the one for parents in Chapter 15. Teachers' opinions are obviously more professional than those of parents, and generally closer to the school. Where parents and teachers agree, problems and concerns are likely to be real (often students, graduates, and taxpayers have similar perceptions). With slight modifications this survey can also be used for other staff members and even the board of education. In the same way that the parent survey encourages responsiveness to the customer, the teacher survey helps to open up communication and participation for staff. It signals to administrators (although you might think this would already be obvious, in an era of collective bargaining) that what the staff thinks, counts and must be considered, listened to, and responded to. Schools are fortunate to have several key groups to ask about problems, concerns, and improvement opportunities, as well as strengths and success. Generally teacher survey results identify more improvement opportunities than do parent surveys, as one would hope. Good performers in any field seldom run out of things that can be improved.

Many of the concepts on the parent survey apply to the teacher survey as well. Questions parallel those in the parent survey almost exactly, except for some slight rewording to adapt them to the viewpoint of teachers. One important additional section covers working conditions, communication, evaluation procedures, and other questions relevant only to teachers.

Many school administrators are not accustomed to operating in this kind of open climate. Schools have been more traditional in their management style, and older principals in particular may find it offensive to think of communication going from their staff members directly to more senior administrators or even to the board. You will want to reassure them that this opening up of communication does not have negative consequences but, rather, provides an early warning system for concerns. Nevertheless, some school administrators, much like factory managers at the turn of the century, will not be able to function effectively under a more open system. Perhaps most important in persuading administrators of the value of this information is its usefulness in setting priorities, providing positive reinforcement for the staff, and actually improving performance. These reasons are so compelling that many administrators now are quite willing to have this kind of information, and some districts are already providing it on a routine basis.

However, I can remember vividly presenting this chapter to a group of principals in the early 1980s and watching one of them turn red as I talked about the values of a parent survey, reported openly to the management team and board. Finally he could restrain himself no longer, and burst out, "My gosh, if you want to get opinions from parents, next you'll probably want to get opinions from teachers!" Of course he was right, but this did not help him feel comfortable with it, and he took an early retirement within a year or two of his district's decision to open up communication.

When interpreting results of the teacher survey, you will need to be a little cautious about the possibility that teachers could choose to gang up on a particular issue or individual. We often suggest that the surveys be conducted during a teacher meeting when 15 or 20 minutes can be devoted to filling them out, and there can be some assurance that teachers are not deliberately skewing results. Some administrators have also worried that unions might try to affect how teachers respond to these survey questions. In practice I have never found this to be a real problem, but I can understand why there might be concerns. Again, having the survey administered during a specific period of time when teachers are together is a way to hedge against this risk.

Interpreting results of the teacher survey is as easy as it is for the parent survey. Simply look down the responses and find those with a high number of "No" answers. For both the parent and teacher surveys we have also tried calculating percentages, but they are not as useful as absolute numbers. You generally have to look back to the real numbers anyway to ascertain whether only a few parents or teachers answered the question, and we find dealing with both percentages and absolute numbers somewhat difficult. While using the three-part answer form "Definitely", "Partially," and "No" does leave some uncertainty as to the distinction between "Definitely" and "Partially," it has the advantage of clearly indicating when "No" is meant.

In the case of teachers even more than of parents, follow-up discussion, often by the superintendent and principal with teachers at a faculty meeting in each school, is clearly desirable. Positive reinforcement for a job well done must be balanced with an effort to find out what is really bothering teachers. It is not uncommon to find a school in which teachers are concerned about several issues, perhaps because the principal has not openly sought their concerns and responded effectively to them. And I have seen whole districts where teacher concerns accumulated over the years, and during the first survey many problems were identified. Sometimes these seem trivial in retrospect—the pothole in the playground, the sticky door to the classroom—but these can be serious impediments to teacher effectiveness and need to be remedied.

In a district that has conducted surveys for many years, it is more likely that relatively few problems will surface, and a survey may be turned to more fine-tuned searching for ways that teachers feel performance can be further improved. Still, periodic surveys provide a useful early warning system and communication vehicle for teachers.

In addition to surveys, the most effective superintendents provide ample time for personal communication. Styles differ, but I know many superintendents who allocate a certain amount of time to spend in each school. Most school districts are small enough to make this feasible, and there is nothing like seeing the boss to have a feeling that someone cares, and the chance to communicate concerns if they exist.

One superintendent meets personally once each year with every teacher in the district. Some years he does this in his office; other years he goes to the schools and does it in a faculty lounge. The teachers of that district surely feel they have access to the top of the organization with whatever problems, concerns, feelings, and attitudes they consider important enough to share.

Of course no system is perfect, and every district is likely to have a few staff members unhappy over any particular issue. The survey provides an extremely useful vehicle for minimizing this unhappiness, and for helping to ensure that communication is open both up and down.

				Don't
I. EDUCATIONAL PROGRAM	**Definitely**	**Partially**	**No**	**Know**
1. In general, I am satisfied with the educational performance of the school in which I teach.	D	P	N	DK

<table>
<thead>
<tr><th></th><th>Definitely</th><th>Partially</th><th>No</th><th>Don't
Know</th></tr>
</thead>
<tbody>
<tr><td>2. The District's academic program
   meets my expectations.</td><td>D</td><td>P</td><td>N</td><td>DK</td></tr>
</tbody>
</table>

3. Students are making satisfactory
   progress (according to ability) in
   the following subject areas:

Reading	D	P	N	DK
Writing	D	P	N	DK
Spelling	D	P	N	DK
Grammar and Punctuation	D	P	N	DK
Mathematics	D	P	N	DK
Social Studies	D	P	N	DK
Science	D	P	N	DK
Music	D	P	N	DK
Art	D	P	N	DK
Physical Education	D	P	N	DK

4. Children have about the right amount
   of homework.   D   P   N   DK
   Or: Too much _____ Too little _____

5. School services are meeting children's
   needs satisfactorily in the following areas:

Special Education	D	P	N	DK
Psychological Services	D	P	N	DK
Speech Services	D	P	N	DK
Social Work Services	D	P	N	DK
Guidance and Counseling	D	P	N	DK
Gifted Education	D	P	N	DK
Chapter I Reading	D	P	N	DK
Bilingual Program	D	P	N	DK
Nursing	D	P	N	DK
Library/Media	D	P	N	DK

	Definitely	**Partially**	**No**	**Don't Know**
6. The schools' athletic programs are appropriate.	D	P	N	DK
7. The schools' extracurricular activities are appropriate.	D	P	N	DK
8. The district computer program:				
Is worthwhile.	D	P	N	DK
Should be expanded.	D	P	N	DK

9. What changes, if any, would you suggest in the Educational Program?

_____

_____

_____

II. SCHOOL/COMMUNITY RELATIONS

	Definitely	**Partially**	**No**	**Don't Know**
1. Cooperation is satisfactory between teachers and:				
Parents	D	P	N	DK
Principals	D	P	N	DK
2. Children are treated fairly in school.	D	P	N	DK
3. Parents are treated well when they visit the school.	D	P	N	DK
4. Student behavior in school is satisfactory.	D	P	N	DK
5. School disciplinary practices are appropriate.	D	P	N	DK
6. The report card used is helpful in communicating children's progress.	D	P	N	DK

	Definitely	Partially	No	Don't Know
7. Parent/teacher conferences are meaningful.	D	P	N	DK
8. Communication between the school and parents is satisfactory .	D	P	N	DK

9. What changes, if any, would you suggest in school/community relations?

_____

_____

_____

III. OTHER SERVICES

	Definitely	Partially	No	Don't Know
1. The Board and Superintendent are fulfilling their responsibilities satisfactorily:				
Board	D	P	N	DK
Superintendent	D	P	N	DK
2. The District is effectively managed.	D	P	N	DK
3. The District spends tax dollars wisely.	D	P	N	DK
4. Student bus services are satisfactory.	D	P	N	DK
5. Student lunch services are satisfactory.	D	P	N	DK

6. What changes, if any, would you suggest?

_____

_____

_____

		Don't
IV. FACILITIES	**Definitely Partially No**	**Know**

1. The district's present school
   buildings are satisfactory in
   size, location and facilities.　　D　　　P　　N　DK

2. The attendance boundaries for
   schools are satisfactory.　　　　D　　　P　　N　DK

3. School buildings are clean
   and adequately maintained.　　　D　　　P　　N　DK

4. Schools have all the books,
   materials, supplies and equipment
   they need for educational
   and other purposes.　　　　　　　D　　　P　　N　DK

5. Concerns or suggestions, if any:

   _____

   _____

   _____

		Don't
V. WORKING CONDITIONS	**Definitely Partially No**	**Know**

1. In general, I am satisfied with my
   teaching position in the District.　D　　　P　　N　DK

2. Working conditions are generally
   satisfactory.　　　　　　　　　　D　　　P　　N　DK

3. Communication is satisfactory
   between teachers and:

   　　Building Administrators　　　　D　　　P　　N　DK

   　　District Office Administrators　D　　　P　　N　DK

4. Trust and confidence is
   satisfactory between teachers and:

   　　Building Administrators　　　　D　　　P　　N　DK

	Definitely	Partially	No	Don't Know
District Office Administrators	D	P	N	DK
5. Staff development opportunities are sufficient and appropriate.	D	P	N	DK
6. The District attempts to be fair to teachers in personnel decisions and policies, and is generally successful in doing so.	D	P	N	DK
7. Teacher evaluation policies and practices are reasonably fair and effective.	D	P	N	DK
8. Teachers have an adequate opportunity to be informed about school programs, policies and practices.	D	P	N	DK
9. Parents and community are supportive of the District and appreciative of its work.	D	P	N	DK
10. District curriculum guides are helpful.	D	P	N	DK

11. Concerns or suggestions, if any:

_____

_____

_____

17

Test Data Analysis: How to Measure and Improve Student Learning

Perhaps the most fundamental principle of organizational effectiveness is the need to clearly establish purpose and measure results. In schools the focus of purpose is on student learning. Fortunately an excellent measure (at least at lower grade levels) is available—standardized achievement test scores. While it is by no means perfect, careful analysis of growth rates and percentiles of achievement compared with ability over a period of at least five to ten years provides a valuable, indeed essential, measure of performance. School boards need to be sure that their administrators are reporting test scores to them in easily understandable formats. Outsiders can also interpret these data—concerned parents or taxpayers, for example. Teachers and administrators should welcome such measures, even though there are some risks, because they are a way of demonstrating good performance, improving results, and justifying funding and salaries.

Test scores are only one indicator of performance, and no one measure of schools is adequate by itself. I have placed this chapter after those on parent and teacher surveys because test scores are less accurate and less complete as a measure. They change from year to year in ways that are sometimes inexplicable. Nevertheless, by measuring results, performance is improved and individual creativity and differences of style and method are encouraged, as long as they produce good results. Test scores are a much more gentle measure then some of the extremely complicated and time-consuming objective-setting techniques imposed by some states on their schools. And be careful not to overmeasure, providing an incentive to fiddle with results. A simple local system is preferable to state-imposed bureaucratic overhead.

In general, the way to analyze test scores is by looking for patterns and trends over time, and by comparing schools, subjects, grades, and classrooms within your own district. The two best indicators for these purposes are growth rates and percentiles of achievement compared with ability.

GROWTH RATES

I find growth rates the most useful single indicator of school performance. In effect, it provides the equivalent of earnings per share for schools. Do not put too narrow a focus on any one indicator, so that schools do not fall into the same trap as some American corporations that have emphasized quarterly improvements in earnings per share instead of overall strategic success in the long run.

Growth rates are calculated by subtracting, for example, last year's fourth grade equivalent score from this year's fifth grade score. The national average growth is ten months per year (corresponding to a ten-month school year). The idea that students should grow one year per year in school is logical and easily understood by all. It is a good way to pinpoint schools, classrooms, subjects, and grades that offer improvement opportunities. If most schools in your district show growth rates of 10 to 12 months per year in school, but one or two show growth rates of 6 or 8 months per year, you can focus your improvement efforts where they are needed.

Growth rates have the attractive feature of equalizing high and low socioeconomic communities. It is actually more feasible to show higher growth rates if your students start out with low achievement scores in the first grade, than if they are already achieving at the third or fourth grade level, as they are in some high-income districts. A problem with both percentiles and grade equivalents is that they vary with the wealth, income, education, and general socioeconomic status of the community. Therefore, above-average communities show above-average test scores. The school board, superintendent, administrators, and teachers may be inclined to stop the analysis right there, in order to achieve the most favorable image and the least risk of sharper comparisons.

To give you some idea of typical ranges of performance, I have seen districts with growth rates as high as 16 months per year and as low as 6 months per year. Three districts have raised their growth rate from 6 months to 12 months annually. In my opinion, every school, grade, and subject should be able to achieve a year's growth for a year in school. Individual classrooms are more difficult to measure, and scores vary more from year to year. Sometimes you even see a negative growth rate if high mobility has caused high-performance students to move out and those with lower achievements to move in. Of course, the reverse can happen. I have seen individual schools with the average growth rates as high as 20 months per year and as low as no growth. Obviously a zero growth rate school has serious problems that need attention. One district I worked with had this kind of pattern in the junior high school; it closed the school and moved the students back to elementary buildings. This has broader social purposes and benefits as well, but it indicates the kind of action that may be required. Another district I worked with found a similar pattern in the sixth, seventh, and eighth grades, which were housed in a building with younger children as well. It decided, on this basis, to build a junior high school; the growth rates at this level have risen considerably.

PERCENTILES OF ACHIEVEMENT

Balance growth rates by looking at percentiles of achievement. Generally, it is reasonable for a district to aim to achieve above the fiftieth percentile and above the level of its IQ scores. However, districts in above-average areas with respect to income and other socioeconomic indicators will almost always be over 50 percent. This is not a good sign in itself. Many districts I have worked with have achieved higher percentiles than their IQ scores would indicate.

Generally speaking, percentiles should be rising through the grade levels rather than declining. I worked with one small district that started out with students in the 80s in the first grade and the 40s by the eighth grade. This is not a good pattern. You may also expect to see percentiles of achievement rising over the years, depending on where they are to begin with. Districts that work hard at identifying and realizing improvement opportunities have achieved substantial improvements in percentile scores. In fact, districts with strongly improving achievement test scores have also, in some cases, been able to achieve an apparently rising pattern of IQ scores as well. Obviously the tests overlap, and what they are really doing is revealing the true IQs of the students because of a strong academic program. I have seen this pattern only in districts starting with disadvantaged or average students. It does not, in my experience, occur in districts that start with above-average students; there, because of high achievement in lower grades, there is less opportunity for improvement in scores over time.

GRADE EQUIVALENTS

Finally, look at grade equivalents. This, I believe, is the least valuable indicator, except that you will need these figures to compute growth rates. These data should parallel percentiles, and you will probably want to be at or above national norm levels and to show a pattern that is rising over the years and grades, as with percentiles. However, these numbers should vary in almost exactly the same way as percentiles, so for simplicity's sake I usually look at growth rates and percentiles, and only secondarily at grade equivalents.

Exhibit 11 presents a basic format for test score analysis. I have used this simple, easy-to-understand format to analyze test scores in hundreds of schools and districts across the country. On the right side of the exhibit are average annual growth rates, expressed in months, for several years. This district (Antioch, Illinois) is achieving a remarkably high rate of growth, one of the highest I have seen, considerably more than a year's growth for a year in school. In the middle section of the exhibit are grade equivalents. This pattern has also been improving, following the percentiles shown on the left. Finally, on the left side are the achievement percentiles of the district, also showing a rising pattern over the years. The national average percentile is 50.

Later in this chapter Exhibit 12 shows one way to analyze test scores at the classroom level. Here, as you can see, it is necessary to take into account only students present for two years of testing. This particular approach focuses on growth rates. It is also possible to analyze percentiles of achievement compared with ability, focusing on students who are not performing up to capacity. My recommendation is to consider classroom-level analysis only in the context of a thorough district- and school-level analysis, because data at this level do vary, and it is necessary to have a solid context within which to view these numbers.

Remember, averages of test scores are more accurate than individual student scores, which can vary considerably from year to year, depending on the mental attitude of the student at the time of the test and many other factors. Also in this chapter are recommendations for student-by-student test data analysis.

CONCLUSIONS

Perhaps the most important thing to remember in analyzing test scores is to look at many years, at least 5 and preferably 10 or 15. A rising pattern over time is a good sign. Be sure these data are being used effectively in your district. The management team needs to spend time on them, and principals should meet with teachers to discuss them. In districts most advanced in performance and management, teachers are supported in the classroom with these data analyzed for them in a simple, easy-to-understand format that documents good performance over the years, and helps to identify improvement opportunities.

To analyze performance data in this fashion, you will find that a

Exhibit 11
Outside Audit Summary Report—Test Score Analysis, Antioch District #34

Grade	Percentiles							Grade Equivalents							Annual Growth (months)						
	2	3	4	5	6	7	8	2	3	4	5	6	7	8	3	4	5	6	7	8	Aver
Reading																					
1984/85	51	54	54	59	51	51	58	2.8	4.1	5.1	6.2	6.9	7.9	10.0							
1985/86	46	55	60	64	55	62	57	2.7	4.2	5.5	6.5	7.2	8.8	9.9	13	14	14	10	19	20	15
1986/87	59	62	55	64	68	66	70	3.2	4.4	5.2	6.5	8.4	9.6	11.0	17	11	10	19	24	22	17
1987/88	58	58	59	64	67	71	83	3.1	4.2	5.4	6.5	8.2	10.1	12.1	10	10	13	17	17	25	15
1988/89	55	64	58	64	62	72	70	3.0	4.5	5.3	6.5	7.9	10.2	11.0	14	11	11	14	20	9	13

precondition is relationships of teamwork, trust, and confidence with the faculty, in contrast with the conflict and fragmentation that has often characterized school districts in recent years. Without this, any analysis of test scores may well be taken as part of the adversarial relationship and bargaining process, or be too frightening to be really effective. You will also need internal management systems that hold administrators responsible for performance and support teachers in this objective. Without a management process, your school system will be like a car without any connection between the engine and the wheels.

I often think of test scores as the school equivalent of the bottom level of Maslow's need hierarchy. Like food, shelter, and basic survival needs, they are something you will probably want to concentrate on if they are not satisfactory. Once they are achieved, you will be able to go on to higher-level objectives. If your school board does not know how your schools' results compare with those of other districts, they are failing in their most fundamental responsibility. Controlling cost is important, but you would be foolish to spend any money without making sure you are getting something back. The main thing you ought to be getting back in schools is student learning. Balance this with periodic surveys of parents and teachers, and you will have a good foundation for board confidence and district performance. This will help your board to be positive in staff relationships, and in recognition, respect, and reward for teachers, making positive salary decisions, and expressing the community's gratitude to the staff for a job well done.

Test score analysis can be a tremendous confidence booster for the board and staff, especially when you add the credibility of an outside audit. This provides essential objectivity, independent judgment, analytical experience, and comparative data. As a result, board confidence is given a solid foundation. This shows up in the bargaining process, salary decisions, budgets, and a general attitude of appreciation—rather than questioning of results and wondering whether taxpayers really are getting their money's worth.

The identification of improvement opportunities reassures the board that the district is moving in a positive direction. For staff, positive reinforcement from proof that a good job is being done, and a focus of attention on areas that can be improved, is a powerful means to improve performance.

Following are a description of classroom test data analysis with recommended forms and procedures, and a summary of student-by-student test data analysis in a child-centered reporting system.

CLASSROOM TEST DATA ANALYSIS

Measuring performance is one of the two most important management requirements of schools today. The other is a more humane and participative style of management. The first step is test data analysis and parent/teacher surveys to monitor results, prove where a good job is being done, provide positive reinforcement for the staff, build confidence of the board and public, and provide a sound foundation for accountability and justification for funding and salaries. The second step is to extend test data analysis to the classroom level. This is vitally important to reach what is obviously the most important level of the organization. It provides appropriate feedback to teachers and an opportunity for them to plan, based on factual information about the composition, strengths, and improvement opportunities of each year's students.

This kind of decentralized measurement affords enormously important opportunities for independent initiative on the part of professionals in any field, as is demonstrated by the importance of profit centers in industry. Teachers deserve no less in the way of sensible, practical, easily understood performance information that specifically avoids excessive time, paperwork, and overhead. However, extending test data analysis to individual classrooms is not without its risks and challenges. Until the system is fully operational, teachers may fail to appreciate that it will eventually provide objective documentation that a good job has been done. When this information accumulates over many years, it is perhaps the most reassuring form of performance information available to teachers. But initially it may be somewhat frightening, especially since most teachers are quite concerned about performance and results, and therefore uneasy about measurement. A second problem is that most teachers, like professionals in many fields, are not completely comfortable with any kind of statistical analysis. Like many salesmen, for example, they may prefer people to numbers, or they may have been more inclined to be accountants. In any field where human relations is the predominant requirement, many individuals may be uncomfortable with almost any kind of quantitative analysis, especially such a delicate and difficult-to-measure process as education.

Taking these factors into account argues for proceeding slowly and carefully to build a practical, positive system. No formula can measure school performance perfectly or completely. Nevertheless, these tools are practical and effective to build confidence, reward staff and improve performance. Exhibit 12 presents the recommended format for classroom test data analysis. This is designed to be simple and practical. It could be automated and extended into subtests.

Three steps are involved in implementation. The first is for teachers to sit down, probably with the principal, in the fall to review individual students, and their past achievements and indicated abilities, for the upcoming fall class list. This might be done before school begins, or early in the fall. It should utilize individual student records as maintained by the district and as provided by the standardized achievement

Exhibit 12
Classroom Test Data Analysis

| | | Beginning of Year | | Projected | | End of Year | | |
| | | | | | | | Actual | |
Student	Ability %	Percentiles	Grade Equivalents	Grade Equivalents	Growth	Percentiles	Grade Equivalents	Growth
John J.	55							
Reading		45	2.6	3.6	1.0	50	3.8	1.2
Math		52	2.9	3.9	1.0	46	3.5	0.6
Language		37	1.7	2.7	1.0	42	3.2	1.5
Mary Q.	48							
Reading		54	3.2	4.2	1.0	58	4.5	1.3
Math		42	2.2	3.2	1.0	50	3.8	1.6
Language		60	3.5	4.5	1.0	58	4.5	1.0

(This format would continue with a listing for each student in the class).

tests. Exhibit 12 provides a way of consolidating that information for an entire classroom. The teacher is then asked to project grade equivalents and growth rates for the year, again in conjunction with the principal. Normally the appropriate expectation is a year's growth for each student in each subject.

During the year the teacher and the principal can discuss progress against the background of this factual information on the composition of each class. Typically, a great deal of variation is found from one classroom to another and from year to year. Often students bunch at the top or bottom of the performance range, or at both ends. And what may seem to be abnormal clumps of over- or underachieving students are in fact commonplace. Teaching strategies and time allocations need to vary in response to these changing circumstances, and this information provides a way of beginning to deal with these issues and putting the teacher in a position of making useful planning decisions at the beginning of the year.

At the end of the year each teacher should be provided with feedback information on the actual performance of the students who have been present for both tests, in the spring of the preceding year and the spring of this year. Typically the best time to report this information to teachers is prior to the beginning of school in the fall. It is usually impractical because of the typical timing of tests and the busy time at the end of school to do this in the spring, but it could be done then or even during the summer. In any event, it should be completed before teachers begin to set growth rate objectives for the coming year, so that they have information on how things worked out last year.

Indications that commonly result from this feedback are the need for a teacher to strengthen teaching effectiveness in certain areas, and/or to increase or reduce time allocations in areas where performance could be seen as either too rapid or not fast enough. Since these factors will vary considerably from teacher to teacher, the principal should assume a coaching function with respect to helping teachers find the most productive and appropriate balance of their own time allocations and skills.

While no formula can measure school performance perfectly or completely, this approach is practical and effective, avoiding excessive time or overhead. However, caution is appropriate. Test scores vary inexplicably from year to year, especially for individual students, and they measure only a small part of the total objectives of a good school. A strong sense of teamwork and support is needed to create an environment in which such analysis is tolerable. There are some pitfalls and challenges to be recognized in classroom test data analysis, yet the benefits are overwhelming, both in improving performance and in documenting with solid evidence that teachers are doing a good job. The contribution to board accountability and justifying the funding needed for good schools and fair salaries is obvious.

It is important that classroom test data analysis be considered in the context of solid district growth rates, grade equivalents, and percentiles as outlined in the outside audit school performance formula. This system should be audited annually to be sure it is providing a solid, accurate, comparable foundation. Otherwise, mobility and the relative inaccuracy of test data at student, school, and classroom levels could lead to inappropriate conclusions—unless they are considered in the context of overall district data, appropriately analyzed.

STUDENT-BY-STUDENT TEST DATA ANALYSIS

The final level in linking boardroom with classroom by using test data analysis is student-by-student record keeping. This should be a simple and manageable child-centered system with the teacher in charge. A second viewpoint should be provided by the principal. Together, teacher and principal should know each child, assess his or her capabilities and achievements, and monitor progress. Data should be recorded, probably on a single page for each child. These records should be collected through the years, so that a third grade student, for example, has pages for recorded scores in kindergarten, first, second, and third grades in the file of the current third grade teacher.

The superintendent should meet with each principal periodically during the year to review results and the process being used to work with teachers. These meetings should reveal a principal's knowledge of virtually every student in the school. Ultimately this is the level that drives improvement and performance.

While this seems to be a simple system, it is not operational in more than 1 percent of the schools in the country. Some teachers and principals are managing on their own. Few have a practical districtwide system that makes sense for this essential function. While it is important to balance test data analysis with surveys of parents and teachers, if there were a single step that would add more learning to America's schools than anything else, it would be implementation of this student, classroom, school, and district test data analysis.

Data can be recorded in a simple format that includes the following:

• Achievement test scores

• Grades

• Placement in reading or math groups

• IQ scores

• Birth data

• Special services

• Any other relevant indicators, such as state testing results, local tests, the level at which the student is working in the district's curriculum or textbook.

It is more important that this is done than that a specific standard format is followed.

Applied nationally, such a simple record-keeping system could add as much as two to three years of learning during eight years of elementary school The board's leverage to cause this improvement comes through superintendent leadership and the outside audit. This is the heart of the management process and performance measurement recommended in this book, that could dramatically increase educational productivity.

18

Other Indicators: Hazards, Cautions, and Pitfalls

In spite of the emphasis I have placed on measuring results, I want to make it perfectly clear in this chapter that there are serious reservations about measurement in education—hazards, cautions, and pitfalls. Ultimately, judgment is required to evaluate the performance of any organization. You cannot reduce such important things to a number. Schools, perhaps most of all, because they deal with such a delicate and important commodity, our children, cannot be measured quantitatively alone, by any indicator or even several indicators.

Be sure to build in plenty of opportunity for judgment on the part of the public, school board, administrators, teachers, and other staff members, as well as students. Let them consider what are the purposes and what are the results in the broadest possible way. The most important and highest level of learning is undoubtedly thinking, writing, analyzing, and other such activities that have no real measure. Poetry and philosophy cannot be quantified. The Socratic dialogue promoted for so many decades by Mortimer Adler is a good example of something not measurable but vitally important. It should be made available to every student at the earliest possible age.

The things that can be measured in school tend to be basics—reading and math, for example; once you measure them, you can move on to other things that are not as measurable. Achievement in all areas may depend more on motivation than on teaching of specific content. The ability of a teacher to motivate a student is mysterious, and often unfathomable, yet it is the real key to all learning and progress.

Classrooms, departments, and schools must be comprehended in total, delving into the sociology of the organization to find what makes it tick, what is happening, what is needed, where it is going. Some of the more recent applications of sociology to schools—by, for example, Michael Rutter, Dan Lortie, and Gerald Grant—are wonderful examples of how insightful, humanistic understanding of an organization can bear upon our grasp of its situation and help turn it in a more productive and positive direction.

I have found from years of experience that the products of the major test companies in the United States are reasonably good when it comes to measuring basic skills in reading and math. If you think about it, there is no reason why these kinds of skills cannot be measured on a standardized test. In other areas, such as science and social studies, the tests, in my opinion, fall a good deal further away from complete measurement, and in some cases they may be counterproductive, measuring knowledge when the analytical process and scientific method are more important. I tend to deemphasize test scores in these areas but to suggest to my clients that they are quite reliable on a group basis in areas like reading and math.

Be careful about putting too much credence in IQ scores. For disadvantaged students I know they tend to produce a lower-than-real score, a result that could well discourage teachers from trying as hard as they might. I have seen districts raise IQ scores from the first to the eighth grade by as much as five to ten points, especially in disadvantaged communities, which suggests that these students' real abilities were masked by their inability to take the test, or to handle the language well enough to figure out the questions.

At the high school level, the measurement job is much more complicated than the test scores described in the previous chapter. The surveys are still relevant and need not be changed much, if at all, to adapt them to high school; but in the area of student learning you are looking at a much more complicated process of assessment. Analyze college entry examination scores and advanced placement results as well as National Merit Scholarships and other prizes and competitions, and results of a district's own internal grading system. Individual departments will be able to assess their own performance in the context of a broader mission, and of trends in their field. Behavior and discipline statistics are also relevant. Exhibit 13 summarizes performance information for high schools.

I have concluded from years of experience that the same requirements exist with respect to key performance indicators in schools that apply to a business's financial statement: a need for outside objectivity, experience, and comparisons. This is provided for business through various financial analysts such as Moody's, Standard & Poor's and Value Line; even the Dow Jones industrial average is an example of a simple indicator of performance. And of course every business of large enough

Exhibit 13
High School Performance Concept and Information

1. STUDENT LEARNING AND DEVELOPMENT

   District Performance Indicators
   —Analysis of SAT and ACT scores and trends.
   —Analysis of AP results.
   —Grading analysis.
   —National Merit Scholars, and other competitions.

   Department Results
   —Local examinations and national tests.
   —Basic skills, as well as higher level thinking and writing, and philosophical debate.

   Behavior and Discipline
   —Dean's reports of attendance, expulsion, suspension and dropout data.
   —Analysis of information with identification of trends and possible implications.

2. CONSTITUENT SATISFACTION

   —Surveys of parents, teachers, students, graduates.
   —Informal discussions and interviews.

3. COST

   —Financial planning and cost control.

size has an audited financial statement on which the board of directors depends for assurance that they are monitoring performance on the basis of realistic year-to-year comparisons. School districts need this same outside objectivity, experience, and comparative database applied to the key indicators of test scores and parent/teacher surveys. The Institute for Public Management has conducted hundreds of these outside audits since 1975.

The test companies have been criticized by some for helping districts show that they are doing a good job when this may not in fact be the case. Recently it has been reported that almost every major American city school system shows improving test scores, and that this may be more a function of clever analysis and presentation than of real improvements. It certainly is not impossible that the test companies are happy to have the tests sold whether or not the results are used.

The most serious criticism I would make, not against the test companies, is that many districts do not make much use of these data. The analysis is somewhat complicated, and you must have several years of data in order to do it correctly. Many districts, possibly even a majority, do not have these numbers together in a way that they can be analyzed correctly. Perhaps because they lack the staff capability or the analytical experience, many districts wind up analyzing the numbers incorrectly, underutilizing them, or simply leaving them on the lengthy computer printouts sent back by the test companies. I have seen individual principals and teachers struggling to put these together in ways that would seem preposterous to an industrial manager whose controller or financial analyst is providing this kind of staff support with respect to key indicators of performance. This same kind of analytical support is needed for analyzing school performance, which is actually more challenging to analyze than business indicators such as return on investment and earnings per share.

A word of caution is also needed on not overanalyzing these numbers. Many states have put more of a time and cost burden on their local districts than is worthwhile in order to comply with state requirements for assessment and objectives. They should have hired an industrial engineer to figure out the cost of compliance before imposing these bureaucratic procedures. Other well-intentioned efforts—like the outcome-based accreditation of agencies such as the North Central Association—have sometimes produced excessive paperwork and too much information rather than meaningful analysis and conclusions. However, some of this is necessary experimentation in the course of finding the right information and analytical procedures.

Performance information is only half of what you need to improve your school. The other half is a management process with planning and evaluation of programs, schools, and departments. For this you will need responsible administrators, and a dialogue between the administrator responsible for each program, school, or department and a central office administrator or committee. This is the management process part of the governance-management-performance system (described in Part VI).

The final requirement is for the board to evaluate the superintendent on the basis of performance information and the management process (described in Part VII).

19

Value and Cost: Financial Planning and Cost Control

The value of good schools is far more important than their cost. However, cost is important. The financial side of education is much too large an issue to cover in a single chapter, so I will share three small points with you. One is an argument for the value of good schools in terms of America's international economic competitiveness and social progress. Second is an anecdote that points out the implications for property values, especially in America's big cities. Third is a model for financial planning and cost control to highlight the major economic factors in schools.

As stated earlier in this book, opportunities to improve the output side of education—student learning, parent satisfaction, public confidence, teacher morale and productivity—are more important than improvement opportunities on the cost side. Most schools, those in big cities excepted, are not top-heavy with bureaucracy. Most of them do a pretty good job of controlling costs in support areas such as buildings, maintenance, food service, school buses, and clerical operations. They are not perfect, and your district may have improvement opportunities, but if you think you are going to achieve substantial changes in the cost of education because of this, you are probably wrong. A major factor, of course, is the number of employees compared with the number of students, and in this respect you may find that fine-tuned analysis can help. I know districts that doubled the staff–student ratio without realizing it, and others who found an extra teacher in each department (just to be sure they were not understaffed after course selections were made).

THE VALUE OF GOOD SCHOOLS

As America and the world economy shift from industrialization and manufacturing to services and information, it becomes obvious that the importance of education is even greater than it was in America's traditional concept of upward mobility. Our growing realization of this lies behind the current school reform movement and especially behind the outpouring of comments from business executives about the importance of schools. When business executives speak out in favor of better schools, they speak from an accurate realization that the quality of America's talent is the single most important determinant of our international economic competitiveness and the health of our domestic economy as well. Education is the means to upward mobility not only for individual families but also for our entire economy.

PROPERTY VALUES OF EFFECTIVE SCHOOLS

In Europe's big cities—Paris and London, for example—the most valuable real estate is at the center, where residential property values allow only the wealthy to live. In America the opposite is true. The main reason is the poor-performing public schools in most big cities. While part of the decline of property values may have stemmed from our success in integration and the disruption this caused in schools during the 1960s and 1970s, it now presents perhaps our greatest single property value improvement opportunity. The potential real estate profits from improving schools in America's big cities are high. We cannot afford not to spend what is needed to achieve this. The nice part is it should not cost any more than what we are spending now, or at least not much more. Examples in this book document that urban communities can achieve growth rates as good as those of the suburbs. If we were to do this in our big cities, the payoff in property values would be stunning.

As an example of how this works, I put three Chicago-area school districts that have achieved substantial performance improvements in urban communities on television in an ABC special called "Schools That Work." Zion, North Chicago, and Hazel Crest are districts that have doubled the rate of student learning from 6 months to 12 months per year. The program also mentioned Antioch, Lake Villa, and Lake Forest, where significant improvements have also been achieved. As I discussed these results with Dr. Dorothy Boyd, superintendent in Hazel Crest, she pointed out that they were having a problem with Chicago mothers who tried to enroll their children in Hazel Crest schools by renting an apartment for just one month, or pretending to live with children's grandparents.

As Dorothy talked, I suggested facetiously that perhaps I should check my liability insurance to see if I was covered for the strain on local taxpayers from citizens of other communities enrolling their children in these schools. Then it occurred to me that perhaps I should just ask for a kickback from the improvement in property values that could come out of the rush to live in an area near Chicago that offers good education. Then it occurred to me to check in Lake Forest, the community where I once served on the school board. I reckoned that roughly $1 billion in property values has accrued since 1972—admittedly much of it coming from inflation—but a good portion from the demonstrably high-quality schools developed in this area by the faculty and staff, management team, and board under the leadership of Dr. Allen J. Klingenberg. I suggested to Al that he should ask for the kind of bonus plan that Lee Iacocca has, in this case based on property values instead of stock prices.

I hope these anecdotes help you to appreciate the tremendous value of good schools for America's economic prosperity and continued social progress. I believe that our national deficit is being caused by America's desire to spend for desirable social ends beyond what we can afford. Management of public services is needed to correct this imbalance. America's civil rights progress has been stalled by the poor quality of our urban schools. The problem is school performance and the ways schools are managed. No amount of welfare, prisons, or even federal troops in the cities will solve the problems. Only good schools can do it.

FINANCIAL PLANNING AND COST CONTROL

The rest of this chapter is a model for financial planning and cost control in schools. It focuses on key cost control factors, the main requirements of financial planning, and board decisions.

School Financial Planning and Cost Control Model

This model is designed for discussion with school boards, superintendents, business managers, and other administrators. The objectives are the following:

• To provide a conceptual framework identifying key components of financial planning and cost control

• To recognize the inherent complexity and uncertainty of school finance, and to focus on the most important factors

- To highlight important board decisions and information
- To help boards and administrators work together to deal responsibly with these difficult issues

  I. *Cost Control—Key Board Policy Decisions:* Considering community needs, desires, and resources, and the educational program to be provided in response, these are the key financial policy decisions that must be made by the board:
     1. *Staff/student ratios*
        - Primary determinant of total costs
        - Importance of control; cost implications, public sensitivity, impact on staff
        - Limited research evidence, often conflicting: a judgment call
     2. *Salaries policy*
        - Teachers, administrators, others
        - Relating compensation to performance
        - Internal equity, external comparisons
     3. *Other Costs*
        - Less important than salary, but must be considered.
        - Aggressive identification of possible cost reduction opportunities
        - Program options
        - One-time gains or expenditures—sales of assets, maintenance, facility requirements
     4. *Tax rate (referendum timing)*
        - First three components total to district budget, indicating tax rate required
        - Timing of referendum to increase tax rate: when funds are required risks of defeat, local circumstances that might affect the likelihood of success
     5. *Cash reserve/debt policy*
        - Outside the basic equation
        - Could cushion uncertainties of financial projections, avoid short-term adjustments in other elements of the equation
        - Need to establish a cash reserve policy
          —Considering debt capacity
          —Holding of working capital by district versus citizens
  II. *Financial Planning—Projections and Assumptions:* These are the key factors in developing school financial projections:
     1. *Enrollment*
        - Rolling forward prior enrollment experience usually produces fairly accurate projections, at least in the short run
     2. *Assessed valuation*
        - Assessment practices appear mysterious; contrasting trends in similar communities seem inexplicable.
        - Past accuracy of local projections should be monitored as an indication of how predictable this factor may be.
     3. *Timing of tax receipts, and allocation of revenues by tax year*

- Might use cash reserves to hedge against variations in the timing of tax receipts.
- As much as six months operating budget might be needed.
4. *State aid*
   - Projections can be based on historical funding or formula projections—both subject to uncertainty.
   - Changing economic circumstances, or adverse political decision making at state level, can have a major impact.
5. *Inflation*
   - Difficult to project
   - Range of alternative possibilities seems essential, such as 5 percent, 10 percent, and 15 percent.
   - Risk of a self-fulfilling impact on teacher expectations
6. *State school finance policy; taxpayer revolt*
   - Most uncertain area of projection
   - Potential swings up or down can be substantial

III. *Decisions, Guidelines, and Cautions:* These are some considerations that may affect board financial decision making:
1. *High level of complexity and uncertainty*
   - Inherent complexity and real uncertainty
   - Judgment, and differentiating between short run and long run, essential
2. *Staff support to board decision making*
   - General strategy for financing the district, with contingencies
   - Analysis and supporting information in all areas identified in this model
3. *A positive rather than negative impact on public confidence and staff morale*
   - Challenging human dimension of financial planning
   - Public and staff sensitive to financial issues
4. *Rationalizing financial decisions to the public and staff*
   - Inherently conflicting interests of teachers, parents, and taxpayers
   - Political and financial equation: difficulties of decisions involving both qualitative and quantitative factors
5. *Separate cost control and financial planning from program and resource allocation*
   - Frightening and confusing to deal with at the same time
   - Natural defensiveness damaging to morale and teamwork
6. *School performance information important*
   - Evidence to show that expenditures were worthwhile
   - Test data—student learning, surveys of parents and teachers
   - Strategy of good performance and cost control

VI

Reward Your Staff: Participative Management Plans

20

Recommended Organization: Participative and Accountable

This chapter contains the summary of an organization plan to implement participative management with performance measures and board accountability. It was recommended to an elementary district of about 4,000 enrollment, adjacent to a major city in a community with a wide range of socioeconomic levels and a mixture of racial and ethnic groups.

As each district goes through the transition from traditional authority to modern participation and responsibility for performance, it is necessary to communicate what this process means. That requires thinking and discussing by the board, management team, faculty, and others in the district.

- What does it mean to accept responsibility for performance?
- What does it mean to have open communication?
- What does it mean to use performance information positively?

These are issues that must be explored and discussed in each district according to its own individual character, circumstances, and situation. An organization plan is one way to help communicate these changes, to provide the common, shared understanding essential to successful implementation.

This chapter is the tip of the iceberg, a summary of the kind of documentation that is needed and the communication that is required, to achieve a successful transition from traditional authority to participation and responsibility for results.

BACKGROUND AND HIGHLIGHTS

The recommended plan is based on a series of meetings with the superintendent; personal interviews with each district administrator; visits to each school; discussions with a representative sample of board members, parents, and teachers; review of district documentation regarding organization, evaluation, compensation, and performance; and experience in hundreds of similar studies for other school districts as well as business and government. These recommendations are for a participative and accountable organization—implemented through a decentralized structure emphasizing communication, teamwork, trust, and confidence among support staff, faculty, administrators, and board. The purpose is to achieve good performance on behalf of the public, with parents and students well served by their schools; taxpayers getting their money's worth; accountability documented with objective information; and a positive, participative process of evaluation that encourages and supports good results with responsibility and teamwork.

This plan is designed to be participative and accountable:

- *Participative* with empowerment of teachers and positive relationships of teamwork, trust, and confidence—communication, recognition, and reward—a supportive management process with performance-driven planning, organization, evaluation, and compensation. This extends to schools the same freedom with responsibility that America successfully pioneered in national government.

- *Accountable* to a demanding community with objective performance information including measures of student learning and development, public confidence and parent satisfaction, teacher morale and job satisfaction, and cost-effectiveness—to prove that a good job is being done, identify improvement opportunities, and win support and appreciation, including the funding needed for good schools and fair salaries. This extends to schools the same pragmatic measures that America pioneered in agriculture and industry, with results that have shown the world how to improve productivity.

Participation and accountability are supported by board policies and superintendent leadership giving staff the freedom and responsibility to achieve and improve upon good performance.

RECOMMENDATIONS

These are recommendations to implement this participative and accountable organization concept:

- The management team should be comprised of four central office directors and ten school principals collectively responsible for district performance, management, teamwork, and accountability under superintendent leadership and board policy.

- Four central office departments are recommended: business, personnel, special education, and instruction. These departments should be service agencies to improve school effectiveness.
- The most substantial change is in the instructional department: a transition from traditional authoritarian school administration with its top-down approach to more participative and results-oriented management.
  —The purpose is to provide positive, effective support for instructional improvement.
  —Teacher leader positions should be used to assure instructional expertise and to provide for necessary administrative responsibility for various subjects and programs.
  —Recommended are the equivalent of two full-time positions, one staffed permanently and the other on a rotating one- or two-year basis, depending on subjects currently under review, plus several part-time positions, appropriately compensated and, where necessary, with adequate released time.
  —These positions are experimental. They straddle the traditional boundary between administration and faculty, to encourage a bottom-up participative approach and more effective results.
  —These positions should be rationalized into a structure that includes other second-level administrative positions, such as assistant principals, building assistants, committee chairpersons, special education administrators, and reading and learning disorder specialists in each school.
  —Specific responsibilities are likely to differ in each subject and program, and should respond to the requirements of that subject and specific functions to be fulfilled. A common dimension is provision of expertise and access to innovative, effective programming and materials in each area.
  —In spite of the heavy leadership responsibilities of principals and inherent time limits, their authority and mentorship may be essential to empowering teacher leader positions.

- Central office special education staff support functions are not materially changed by the recommended organization, but should be reconsidered in light of changes in the instructional department.
- The personnel function should be strengthened to provide more time for staff recruitment and selection in support of principal (and faculty) decision making, with more aggressive central office evaluation and screening. To make possible this strengthening, one additional secretarial position should be authorized.
- Business department functions are minimally impacted by these recommendations. There is a need to reallocate responsibilities in some areas, to continue improvement of procedures already initiated, and to respond to community needs for confidence in financial planning and cost control.
- Substantial reductions in central office administrative positions (from 13 to 4) should be balanced by 1 or 2 additional secretarial personnel in the superintendent's office and/or shared with the personnel or instructional departments.

Implementation Steps

Four steps should be carried forward immediately:

• Detailed organization planning within these recommendations
• An administrative compensation plan (outlined below)
• An administrative evaluation plan (outlined below)
• Performance information, to provide the necessary objective documentation, including parent/teacher surveys and test data analysis.

Organization. Job descriptions are needed for the board of education, superintendent, and management team. Each central office director should detail administrative and secretarial staffing, organization, and responsibilities within the framework of these recommendations.

Compensation. An administrative compensation plan should be prepared.

• Analytical comparisons have already been initiated. With this evidence, the board should consider how administrative salaries currently relate to the market—and how they should relate.
• Categories, targets, and ranges should provide a more solid basis for the board's administrative compensation decisions and improve recognition and reward for administrators.
• The emphasis should be on the quality of district performance delivered by the entire management team, rather than on individual competitiveness.
• Compensation should be justified by performance and the quality of the educational program being delivered, considering both educational results and taxpayers' return on their investment. Performance criteria should include the following:
  —Student learning and development
  —Parent satisfaction and public confidence
  —Teacher morale and job satisfaction
  —Administrative procedures, and cost-effectiveness.

Evaluation. Administrative evaluation policies and procedures should be specified in a formal plan, to provide a foundation for the confidence and delegation essential to participative management, and to guarantee accountability for board and public.

• The present goal-setting and review process by the superintendent with each principal should be built upon as the core of administrative evaluation.
• Performance information should be added in the form of parent/teacher surveys and test data analysis including an outside audit.

- Both process and information should be reported to the board, to assure their understanding of performance, improvement, process, and results.
- Criteria should stress performance and teamwork, with emphasis on responsibility and improvement.

Administrative evaluation should be grounded in a planning process beginning with a realistic assessment of the situation in each school and department.

Information. Objective performance information is essential for board/ staff accountability and teamwork. It is a vital enabling step for participative management, the foundation for board confidence and delegation, improving performance, and demonstrating that taxpayers are getting their money's worth. Naturally, caution and judgment must be exercised in using performance information to evaluate such a complicated enterprise as a school. Multiple indicators are essential, starting with feedback from parents and teachers, and including analysis of test scores and other indicators of student learning.

- The district should adopt a concept of performance and make more effective use of information to support its achievement and improvement.
- The teacher survey should be strengthened and a parent survey should be added in a parallel format.
- Analysis of standardized achievement scores should be brought up to date and strengthened in formats and procedures.
- An outside audit should assure credibility, considering data in the context of trends and patterns in other districts.

Performance information should be used effectively and positively to support participative management, teamwork, and shared responsibility as well as individual contributions.

Exhibits 14 and 15 are the recommended district and central office organization charts.

Exhibit 14
Recommended District Organization

Community

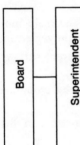

Board

Superintendent

Management Team

Accountability to the public for district performance, management, and teamwork

Overall district leadership and board support for teamwork, accountability, performance, and management

Directors (4)

. Central office personnel including assistant administrators and secretarial staff

. Business—financial planning, cost control, and management of supporting services

. Personnel—recruitment, selection, evaluation, development and compensation of staff

. Instruction—leadership for instructional improvement and district-wide monitoring of performance

. Special Student Services—management of special education programs and other specialized services

Principals (10)

. School staff including assistant principals, building assistants, teacher leaders, teachers, aides, secretarial, custodial and food service personnel.

. Direct responsibility for:

— Student learning and development in line with district objectives and community needs

— Parent satisfaction and public confidence

— Teacher morale and job satisfaction

— Administrative procedures

Exhibit 15
Recommended Central Office Organization

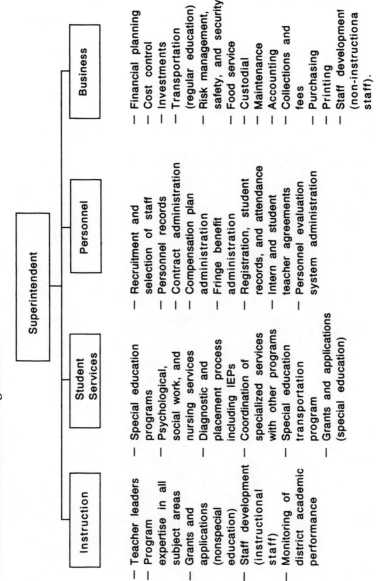

Superintendent

Instruction

— Teacher leaders
— Program expertise in all subject areas
— Grants and applications (nonspecial education)
— Staff development (instructional staff)
— Monitoring of district academic performance

Student Services

— Special education programs
— Psychological, social work, and nursing services
— Diagnostic and placement process including IEPs
— Coordination of specialized services with other programs
— Special education transportation program
— Grants and applications (special education)

Personnel

— Recruitment and selection of staff
— Personnel records
— Contract administration
— Compensation plan administration
— Fringe benefit administration
— Registration, student records, and attendance
— Intern and student teacher agreements
— Personnel evaluation system administration

Business

— Financial planning
— Cost control
— Investments
— Transportation (regular education)
— Risk management, safety, and security
— Food service
— Custodial
— Maintenance
— Accounting
— Collections and fees
— Purchasing
— Printing
— Staff development (non-instructiona staff).

21

Administrative Compensation: Based on Performance

This chapter includes the summary of a recommended plan of performance-based administrative compensation. The purpose is to support board accountability with compensation based on performance that is fair to administrators. The board should use performance-based compensation to be sure that taxpayers are getting their money's worth and to support performance improvement, management development, and teamwork. The heart of the plan is a concept of fair salaries and positive relationships offered by the board to administrators in exchange for performance information and evaluation proving that a good job is being done and identifying improvement opportunities. Administrative compensation is a critical issue in the management transition required in every district by the new circumstances of education. In many districts administrators have come to feel less well protected and less well compensated compared with teachers. The approach recommended in this chapter is designed to support teamwork and accountability: to provide a sound foundation for board decisions, and to assure fairness to administrators.

The recommended plan emphasizes responsibility for and delivery of good performance, justifying salaries and budgets on this basis. This is the only responsible (and politically salable) justification in an era of board assertiveness and public concern about school performance and accountability. This system is also designed to offset personal opinions of the board and superintendent with objective evidence of good performance. Thus administrators are given some of the same protections that teachers have won through union contracts, yet in a system that is performance-based and can be used to justify fair salaries and adequate budgets. It builds teamwork, trust, and confidence—with positive reinforcement in an upward spiral of improvement—instead of conflict and decline.

Often administrative compensation is the first signal that a district is entering the transition to a new style of management. This is manifested in the board's unwillingness to approve superintendent recommendations for administrative salaries. Typically, these recommendations were made by the superintendent without any formal system, and approved by the board without debate. As this era has come to an end, many superintendents have found themselves still arguing with their boards at two or three o'clock in the morning. Some leave the meeting without administrative salaries approved for the coming year. The solution to this immediate problem is a more systematic way of setting administrative salaries, such as that described in this chapter. However, even more important, this can be the fulcrum for initiating the transition to participative and results-oriented management. Thus administrative compensation has an importance beyond the fact that administrators are not likely to work without salaries.

In order to move toward performance-based administrative compensation, you must deal with the more difficult question of administrative evaluation. Three exhibits at the end of this chapter describe the components and process we recommend. One key is the performance information described in Part V of this book. Another is the process of planning and evaluation described in Part VII.

Performance-based compensation is a valuable lever for change and improvement, insisting upon responsibility for and delivery of good performance by administrators in exchange for fair salaries, recognition, and reward. These key components are required:

- Board policies for teamwork and success, communication and participation, accountability, good performance, and improvement
- A concept of organization and management stressing teamwork, communication, and responsibility for performance
- A compensation plan based on performance with analysis of internal and external equity and a structure of categories, targets, and ranges
- Performance information including test data analysis, surveys of teachers and parents, and an outside audit
- A planning and evaluation process that applies superintendent judgment to the situation, progress, and objectives in each school and department.

Especially important is the balance between superintendent judgment, with its inherent risks of personal interpretation and the unavoidable turnover of boards and superintendents, and the advantages of objective information to prove continued good performance of long-serving, dedicated teachers and administrators.

This management plan for evaluation and compensation of administrators is based on performance. It strives for a balanced emphasis on fairness to staff and accountability to the public.

ADMINISTRATIVE EVALUATION

Evaluation should be based on three factors:

- Achievements and results should be compared with responsibilities and objectives, through superintendent judgment. This should build upon the process of periodic review meetings conducted by the superintendent with each administrator. Job descriptions, the planning process, and performance information should provide documentation, along with the superintendent's reporting to the board.
- Performance information should be completed as soon as possible—in order to provide a sound basis for board confidence and accountability, assure fairness to administrators, and justify budgets and salaries. This should include parent and teacher surveys and test data analysis, as well as surveys of students and graduates.
- Personal development of each administrator should be considered and encouraged.

POLICIES AND OBJECTIVES

The plan is designed to provide fairness to administrators, a sound and appropriate structure for board decision making, control of administrative salaries on behalf of the public, and maximum contribution of administrative compensation expenditures to overall educational quality, performance, and cost-effectiveness, as well as motivation, morale, performance, productivity, and job satisfaction of administrators and staff.

CATEGORIES, TARGETS, AND RANGES

The plan is organized into categories, targets, and ranges.

- Categories provide for internal equity by grouping positions with responsibilities of similar value.
  - —These categories correspond in general to market distinctions and reflect differences in internal responsibilities.
  - —Adjustments in categories should be made if organization or responsibilities change.

- Target midpoints for each category reflect market analysis.
  —Market comparisons help to establish external equity by comparing district salaries with those for similar responsibilities in other districts.
  —The board should decide how district salaries should relate to the market.

- Ranges for each category establish an appropriate minimum and maximum to reward good performance over time, as it is achieved and demonstrated.

OPERATING PROCEDURES

Placement of individual administrator salaries within ranges should generally follow these guidelines:

- Beginning salaries for new appointments should normally be within the bottom portion of the range, below the target level. Exceptions should be considered where an unusually young manager is promoted or an unusually senior person is required to fulfill a position. All individuals in each category should be expected to be earning at least the minimum salary designated.
- The top of each range provides a maximum salary for positions in the category. Individuals who have spent several years in a position with good performance should expect to be at or above the target level—and, with outstanding performance and long service, in the upper part of the range.
- With good performance, individuals whose salaries are below the target level for the range would expect to move up relatively more rapidly than those above the target level. This is consistent with the usual period of time required to develop good performance in a position.

These procedures should be followed for the board's annual administrative salary decisions:

- Early in the year the board should consider superintendent recommendations for the total budget to be allocated for administrative salary increases.
- Within this framework, the board should delegate to the superintendent responsibility for specific salary recommendations.

Two features of the recommended plan deserve particular attention: fairness to administrators and sound board decision making:

- Fairness to administrators is provided through the structure of the plan and delegation to the superintendent.
- Board control of administrative salaries through a sound decision-making process is provided.

Tying administrative salaries to performance is a positive, constructive use of the board authority for setting salaries delegated to it by the public—for accountability, fairness to staff, and encouraging and rewarding good performance.

IMPLEMENTING RECOMMENDATIONS

Exhibit 16 presents specific implementing recommendations for one district, including categories, targets, and ranges. Exhibit 17 summarizes the key components of administrative evaluation, which are also discussed in Part VII.

Exhibit 16
Administrative Compensation Plan

These are 1988/89 salaries, in thousands of dollars. Categories reflect the internal evaluation exercises and outside market comparisons. Midpoints are geared primarily to county averages. Annual updating to reflect expected market increases would begin this spring. Some immediate adjustments are required to implement the plan. Ranges have been calculated at 30% of the midpoint.

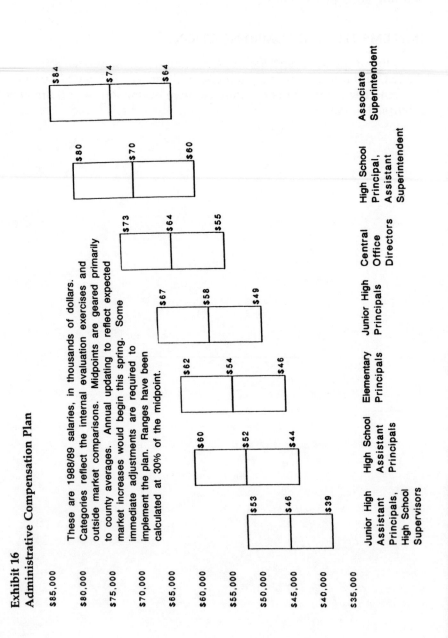

Exhibit 17
Key Components of Administrative Evaluation

I. SUPERINTENDENT JUDGMENT
- Based on responsibilities, objectives, and performance
- Process of dialogue and discussion with each principal
- Considering local circumstances
- Stressing teamwork and responsibility
- Process and results reported to the board (to build confidence).

Unavoidably dependent on personal judgment, reputation/image of principals, incidents involving board members, rumors, and so on.

II. OBJECTIVE INFORMATION
1. *Student Learning/Test Data Analysis*
   - Five to ten years of data in a consistent standardized format for the district and each school, subject, and grade
   - Including percentiles, grade equivalents, and growth rates
   - General standard of a year's growth for a year in school
   - Outside audit to ensure consistent format, analytical experience, comparative reference, outside objectivity
   - Measuring basic skills, recognizing limitations of tests.

2. *Surveys of Constituent Satisfaction*
   - Parent surveys every three to five years
   - Parallel teacher surveys on a similar schedule
   - Surveys of students and graduates.

Long-term measures of basic performance, independent of board or superintendent turnover.

22

Teacher Evaluation: Positive, Fair, and Effective

This chapter includes an example of a plan for teacher evaluation, with definition of responsibilities, a positive approach emphasizing development, and separation of positive evaluation from dismissal or disciplinary proceedings. The purpose is to support leadership toward positive and effective teacher development. Teacher evaluation is one of the most challenging and difficult aspects of school management. Traditionally teachers were evaluated by principals and superintendents who had unfettered authority to dismiss anyone they felt was incompetent or to take whatever disciplinary or corrective action they felt was appropriate. Certainly this was an unfair approach that could not be tolerated in the late twentieth century.

Teacher unions objected effectively and conclusively. In most districts, as a result, evaluation stopped completely. Administrators lacked traditional authority or a more modern system developed and implemented participatively with teachers. So in many districts there was no evaluation, and the normal rate of incompetence, which seems to run about 1 percent of the people in any field, began to accumulate. Teachers who lost their effectiveness with advancing years, who had some personal problem that they could not overcome, who found they liked teaching and were effective for a few years but tired of it—the kinds of problems that often lead to teachers having to be corrected or dismissed—were not being resolved. These poor teachers accumulated, especially in large districts where unions were strongest and administrators hid behind tenure and contracts and what they said was the impossibility of evaluating teachers.

Only a handful of districts across the country overcame these problems with fair evaluation systems that were implemented in practice. In these few cases teachers welcomed fair evaluation, and the good performance and confidence to which it leads, as well as the sound basis it provides for fair salaries and adequate budgets.

This chapter describes one such plan, in a highly abbreviated form. Effective teacher evaluation systems are necessarily somewhat complicated. At the end of the chapter is an outline of key factors that we have found common to these effective plans, along with some general observations.

GUIDELINES

In many districts, teacher evaluation has been rendered inoperative by unions demanding fairness, and rightly so. Consequently, teacher evaluation is not really working, although it may still exist on paper. Successful plans are most often characterized by these features:

- Participative involvement of teachers in designing the plan
- Board, administrator, and teacher relationships of communication, participation, teamwork, trust, and confidence
- A well-defined job description for teachers
- A well-documented plan that spells out procedures and purposes so that teachers can understand and accept them
- Positive evaluation for development separate from that required where dismissal or disciplinary action is needed
- Multiple views, so that evaluation does not depend on a single person or relationship
- Dialogue and discussion between teachers and evaluators aimed at improvement
- Individualized staff development supported by the district
- Positive support for development with the investment justified by improved performance.

Do not try to start with teacher merit pay. Communication, evaluation, and information are prerequisites. But do base total board budget decisions, and administrative compensation, on performance.

These guidelines for positive, fair, effective teacher evaluation are based on interviews with teachers and on research at the Kohl Teacher Center and on my experience interviewing teachers and designing teacher evaluation plans for individual districts.

SUMMARY OF THE TEACHER EVALUATION PLAN

The heart and soul of any service organization is its people. While students, parents, taxpayers, and the entire community contribute to the character and quality of a school district, no more important a role is played than that of the district's faculty, even including the leadership of the board of education, superintendent, principals, and other administrators. How faculty performance is evaluated is central to job satisfaction, personal development, and quality of performance, as well as the total productivity of the district in learning, confidence, morale, and cost-effectiveness. No management function is more important than evaluation and development of teachers. Yet teacher evaluation is often the least-developed management function in schools. It is the one most negatively impacted by recent antiauthoritarian trends (no matter how justified in their own right). It is the most significant opportunity for improvement. It is essential to adequate teacher recognition and reward for good performance.

This plan seeks to address these issues. It is a positive, practical, successful approach to improvement and development. It is aggressive with respect to positive support of good performance for each teacher in the district. It seeks to provide leadership so that teachers can perform at the highest level of which they are capable. The plan is designed to support teamwork and accountability—with good performance in learning, confidence, morale, and cost-effectiveness—and with good management in communication, information, and evaluation.

Job Description and Evaluation Criteria

The first requirement for evaluation is a clear definition of responsibilities. The profession of teaching almost defies definition in the enormous scope and potential of its responsibility, its long-term impact on students, and the possibility of a wide variety of styles and methods to achieve these objectives. Nevertheless, each district needs to produce a concrete definition of its expectations of teacher performance—in order to have a sound basis for teacher understanding, agreement, and acceptance, and for evaluation. A teacher job description is at the end of this chapter.

Observation

Observation of teachers in the act of teaching is a central feature of evaluation, and one of the most important aspects of effective schools.

- The management team should be asked to prepare a list of steps for teacher observation during the coming year.
- Beyond the job description included in this plan, there is also a detailed list of evaluation criteria.
- It is recommended that the management team and faculty consider all effective research that bears upon teacher behavior and its correlation with student learning and development.

Remediation

This is an unavoidably negative part of the evaluation process. It is a distinctly minor yet nevertheless important aspect of the process recommended in this plan. Distinguishing between positive evaluation for development and the inherently negative possible disciplinary action or dismissal that could result from the remediation process is facilitated by structuring the recommended process in three distinct categories:

1. Positive evaluation for development
2. Probationary evaluation
3. Possible disciplinary action or dismissal.

In Category 3, the primary emphasis should be on fully meeting, and exceeding, all due-process requirements.

As in the case of observations, it is recommended that the district management team prepare a specific schedule for remediation steps, including the decision-making process, for those teachers who would be subjected to this. It would be unlikely that more than one to three teachers would be so considered during the course of a year.

Teacher Development and Evaluation Process

This part of the evaluation plan recommends a positive, constructive process of teacher development and evaluation—to improve performance in learning, confidence, and morale; to support board accountability; and to encourage staff relations of teamwork, trust, and confidence. The process should include these component parts:

- Initiation of evaluation by the individual teacher through consideration of his or her own strengths and weaknesses and developmental opportunities
- Dialogue and discussion with the principal and another administrator, possibly in a committee format
- Contribution of outside observations by the principal and/or others
- Recommendation of an individualized development program funded by the

district, initiated and accepted by the teacher, and reviewed and approved by the committee.

The recommended process is designed to support continuing teacher growth and the improvement of student learning and instructional quality. The emphasis is on the teacher's professional responsibilities, with an attitude that is constructively self-critical and aimed at growth, including self-evaluation and district support. Successfully implemented, the process should improve performance, teamwork, and accountability. It will help support district objectives for the success of students in high school and later, the reputation of the district in the community, and its ability to attract students in competition with private schools.

Teacher Job Description

The job description is to help develop understanding of teacher responsibilities, improve performance, and encourage teacher growth and development. It should be discussed, and expanded in more detail, with faculty participation. This concept of performance is also the framework recommended for the district planning process, performance information, and administrative evaluation—to encourage teamwork.

I. Student Learning, Development, and Achievement

1. *Analysis of situation, progress, and expectations*
   - Analyze the potential and progress of each child
   - Project appropriate expectations for each child and each classroom
   - Review and discuss with principal
   - Set goals and objectives annually, with principals

2. *Teaching style and techniques, methods and materials*
   - Match style to children's needs
   - Use appropriate techniques, methods, and materials
   - Exhibit knowledge of subject matter

3. *Student behavior and discipline*
   - Manage student behavior and discipline in the classroom
   - Contribute appropriately to school discipline and behavior
   - Reinforce positive student behavior, encourage self-direction and self-discipline, within school and state codes and policies

4. *Student relationships, assignments, evaluation, and participation*
   - Develop positive student relationships, cooperation, and respect
   - Provide assignments and evaluation appropriate to each child
   - Provide for student initiative, involvement, and participation

5. *Classroom management, learning environment, and social climate*
   - Organize the instructional process effectively
   - Maintain an effective learning environment and social climate
   - Contribute to school environment and climate

6. *Instructional planning and preparation*
   - Plan effectively for instruction, following district curriculum
   - Prepare and use lesson plans (due each Friday)

7. *Individualizing instruction*
   - Individualize instruction to meet the needs of each child
   - Help each child achieve his or her maximum potential

8. *Effectively using special services*
   - Draw upon services outside the classroom appropriately—principal, secretary, nurse, psychologist, social worker, others.
   - Call upon special education services and placements appropriate to meet the needs of individual children

9. *Accomplishments in student learning, development, and achievement*
   - Accomplish basic skills learning progress for each child appropriate to needs and expectations
   - Develop thinking, writing, problem-solving, analyzing, and creative skills and talents as fully as possible

II. Parent Satisfaction and Public Confidence

1. Assure effective communication between teacher and parents
2. Develop a friendly, constructive relationship with parents that helps to meet the needs of each child
3. Contribute to public confidence and parent satisfaction with classroom, school, and district

III. Teacher Relations and Teamwork

1. Maintain helpful, constructive relations with other teachers and with administrators
2. Participate in district responsibilities, such as meetings and committees, and, if possible, provide leadership
3. Contribute to building morale
4. Plan and carry out a program of self-development, with district support
5. Contribute to the development of other teachers, if possible, including serving in a coaching and counseling role if requested
6. Contribute to faculty morale, satisfaction, and productivity

IV. Other

1. Maintain good attendance and punctuality
2. Maintain adequate records and procedures, such as student attendance,

plans for substitutes, report cards, grade book (final information book
to be turned in at year's end)
3. Contribute to program development and advancement of education and
teaching
4. Contribute to building and district objectives

OTHER OBSERVATIONS ON TEACHER EVALUATION

The following comments have been excerpted from a report of observations of effective teachers in high schools prepared for Dr. Jean L.
Damisch. (Thanks to Jean and to Dolores Kohl, both outstanding teachers, for giving me the opportunity to prepare these observations.)

Without measures of results, it is neither useful nor possible to analyze techniques. Creativity and good performance are encouraged by
looking at end results. It would be difficult, if not impossible, to make
observations about techniques without knowing if the players were
successful, if the team won the game, if the students learned and were
satisfied with the development and improvement they experienced as
a result of these classes. This performance information would have to
take two forms. One is objective information on how much the students learned: an achievement test, a written example of work graded
by someone other than the teacher, the Canadian diploma or the English "A" and "O" level, AP (advanced placement) or International
Baccalaureate exams, or someone's judgment, such as that of a principal. Second would be feedback from the students and graduates. I would
like to listen to them discussing a teacher and what they liked and did
not like; or, if that were not possible, then to have some kind of survey.

Then a longer period of observation would be necessary, with
knowledge of the subject matter and the plans for the department and
school. For that, I would need a situation analysis for the school and
department; the perspective of someone responsible, probably the department chairperson; and probably some input from the school level.
I know this sounds complicated and time-consuming, but without it I
do not think any sense could be made of technique and performance.
Probably a series of observations would be needed this year, and the
perspective of at least several previous years. Then a group would need
to sit down with this information and perspective, and put together,
with participation of the teacher, suggestions for improvement and
techniques that might be worth emulation by other teachers.

Each teacher, like an actor or professional in any field, must develop
a personal style. Acceptance of suggestions from anyone else, even an
openness to those suggestions, may impede the development of that
style. In fact, one learns to ignore inferior techniques, and to select

only from people whom one considers superior, in any professional field. Thus the teacher would have to respect the coach, and be willing to accept advice, particularly on such a sensitive and delicate subject as performance. I cannot help commenting here on the relative weakness of department heads in measuring up to these standards, a weakness exacerbated by the wedge that unions have driven into organizations, often between the first level of supervisors and teachers. I am not saying unions were wrong to stop traditional authoritarian practices, just that nothing has taken their place, so that there is not really any process of development and improvement. I feel this is especially true in high schools, where performance improvement has lagged behind other levels of education.

The net of all this, as my research at the Kohl Teacher Center and in individual districts has led me to conclude, is that if teacher evaluation is going to be useful, a much better job is going to have to be done, replacing the virtual absence of anything constructive in most districts at the present time. This is a fundamental key to improving school performance. And the experience of other fields, such as agriculture and industry, suggests that money spent on this would be a good investment. The minimum criteria are the following:

- Measures of student progress
- Dialogue with students (and perhaps parents and other teachers) about the teacher's style and effectiveness
- Feedback from graduates
- An ongoing dialogue between the teacher and a person or a small committee functioning as a coach, to monitor progress and encourage development
- Dialogue and discussion regarding student progress between the teacher and someone else, individualized to each student, probably at least several times during the year
- A coach respected by the teacher whose advice can be at least partially and/ or occasionally accepted—someone with a good, solid, up-to-date knowledge of the subject area and the most effective teaching techniques, who has observed many teachers and has an understanding of the strategic plan for improvement of the school and department, and particular circumstances at both levels, as well as knowledge of this teacher, and his or her personal circumstances, objectives, development needs, and opportunities
- Provision for staff development, preferably on an individualized basis responding to conclusions of the teacher and coach/committee about appropriate improvement opportunities for this individual in the context of this department and school. While some investment is likely to be required, this is usually not very costly. Often the most effective techniques are relatively inexpensive, such as observation of other teachers or an informal seminar conducted by a teacher who has mastered a particular technique and is able to share it with others.

This is a tall order. But it could be the one key step to getting real improvement out of all the national effort that is going into school restructuring and reform.

After all, what is the productivity of a school but the sum total of individual teachers' effectiveness, perhaps multiplied where a strong sense of purpose and mission is involved? In elementary schools we have seen as much as three years added to student learning growth during eight years in school in ten pilot districts. But I do not think comparable improvement is occurring in high schools. One of the reasons is that the management process, particularly teacher evaluation, is sometimes almost nonexistent. If you could help loosen the authoritarian administrative style that still seems to characterize America's high schools, replacing it with more participative and results-oriented management, that would be a marvelous contribution to the effectiveness of teachers and to the quality schools that America needs for its future progress and success.

VII

Evaluate Your Board:
Teamwork, Accountability,
and Success

23

Accountability Plan: Responsibilities and Relationships

Local democracy is the oldest and finest form of public service. School boards are America's best expression of this tradition. American school boards have a unique opportunity today to contribute to our future progress and success by accomplishing the following:

• Giving America the quality schools we need to support our economic success and social progress into the twenty-first century
• Supporting America's economic competitiveness in a world economy of information and services, by assuring that we have the talent we need
• Turning around urban decline, eliminating the underclass, restarting civil rights progress, and adding economic competitiveness to equal opportunity.

While there are significant improvement opportunities in suburban and rural schools, the most important and substantial opportunity is in America's big cities, where poor school performance is causing the underclass, urban crisis, and depressed property values. Good schools could reverse the process. Fortunately, school boards are responding positively to these challenges. They are moving away from traditional authoritarian school administration, where boards were merely rubber stamps for an all-powerful superintendent, to participative and results-oriented management that is improving student learning and satisfying teachers, parents, and taxpayers.

Previous chapters have described this transition and the management requirements it is creating. The focus of this chapter is on board and superintendent responsibilities and relationships—how the board through its own behavior can have a powerful impact on district performance and management while helping to build teamwork and accountability. The most important factor is evaluation of district performance. This concept has two key components. One is the evaluation process. The superintendent should appraise each administrator based on objectives, responsibilities, and results, and report this appraisal to the board. Traditionally this was done by the superintendent in almost total secrecy, with no reporting to the board, or at best with checklists of administrative skills and traits. As you can see, the change is substantial, and it has not been easy for either administrators or superintendents.

The second part is equally difficult—information on school performance: clear analysis of achievement tests and periodic surveys of parents and teachers, with an outside audit to help analyze this information with credibility, experience, perspective, and comparisons. This, too, is a dramatic change for schools from a era of secrecy, when this information was almost never shared with the board, at least not in an understandable form. Administrators would turn red at even the suggestion that parents and teachers should be asked for their opinions in a straightforward, clear-cut survey, the results of which would be published. Nevertheless, districts that have adopted this approach are finding that this information is exactly what is needed to forestall board overinvolvement in administrative details, to build confidence and support, to convince taxpayers that they are getting their money's worth, and to win the funding needed for fair salaries and adequate budgets for schools. Districts with performance information are able to prove that administrators and teachers are earning their salaries, doing a good job, and deserving of respect, gratitude, and appreciation. Nothing is more important to good performance and constructive relationships.

Implementing these two steps in your district will not be easy. First you will need the understanding and leadership of your superintendent; without this do not even bother to try. Then he or she will need to convince administrators that these steps are unavoidable. Frankly, no one is likely to volunteer to be evaluated, partly on the basis of objective performance information, if it can be avoided. The board or superintendent or both must make this a condition of employment. And they must recognize the heavier responsibilities this implies for administrators as well as teachers, and develop the recognition, reward, respect, appreciation, and teamwork, trust, and confidence required. If these conditions are met, implementation is feasible and will result in better performance, more job satisfaction, higher confidence and morale, and significant improvements in student learning.

There are three main things school board members can do to improve performance and management at this delicate but powerful interface between the board and superintendent:

- Make sure that you have a few key indicators of performance clearly analyzed and presented to the board: test data to indicate student learning and parent/teacher surveys to indicate their satisfaction and concerns.
- Make sure the superintendent is actually evaluating administrators, which you should be able to judge from his or her reports of the process and results to the board.
- Build a climate of teamwork, appreciation, and support for good performance through board policies and behavior.

If every school board in America were to take these three steps, the positive contribution to school performance and management would be very substantial.

Finally, a note of caution. While measuring performance is important, Americans have recently discovered in both agriculture and industry that a broader concept of results is also needed. It would be nice if schools could avoid the mistakes that a narrow focus on indicators of performance can encourage. Quarterly earnings per share are not an adequate measure of corporate contribution to product quality, employee productivity and job satisfaction, and customer needs and desires. A broader concept is obviously essential—the impact of the company on the environment and community must be taken into account as well. Similarly, the wonderful productivity of American agriculture is now being recognized as slightly but significantly marred by chemicals that may be doing more harm than good. Obviously we would not want to give up the overall productivity of America's farms and factories, but broadening our social consciousness and performance measures is certainly appropriate—indeed, it is essential.

In schools, it would be nice if we could add performance measures that would drive up our productivity without overemphasizing these factors or narrowing the focus too sharply. Many districts will outgrow the usefulness of standardized achievement tests as their performance rises, with most of the students topping out on the tests. Then their objectives can turn to loftier purposes, such as thinking and writing, or philosophy and the behavioral sciences, subjects that used to be reserved for college-level study that ought to be available at lower grade levels as well.

Because I have seen such dramatic differences in performance as measured by test scores and surveys, even in similar districts near each other, I know that school boards could make a tremendous contribution to the overall productivity of American education if they monitored these key indicators closely.

HOW TO MONITOR PERFORMANCE

Here is a summary of how to monitor performance using both the hard data of performance information and the soft data of an evaluation process. The percentages on the right contrast this recommended plan with the typical historical pattern in schools, which relied almost entirely on checklists of skills and traits and almost not at all on responsibilities, objectives, or performance information.

RECOMMENDED ADMINISTRATIVE EVALUATION COMPONENTS
How boards can monitor performance to justify salaries.

	Recommended Plan— Approximate Weighting	Typical Historical Pattern
Soft Data—Evaluation Process		
This is a process depending primarily on superintendent leadership, judgment, observation of administrators, and willingness to evaluate.		
— Analysis of results, considering the situation and circumstances in each area	20%	0%
— Personal assessment by the superintendent of strengths/improvement opportunities (and value/contribution to the district) for each administrator	15%	0%
— Achievements compared with objectives	10%	0%
— Achievements compared with responsibilities (job descriptions)	5%	0%
— Checklists of administrative skills, traits, etc. (optional)	--	100%
	50%	
Hard Data—Performance Information		
Performance data should be analyzed annually for test scores and every three to five years for surveys (mainly on a group basis for the management team and staff)—with the assurance of credibility, accuracy, analytical experience, and comparisons provided by an outside audit.		
— Test data analysis	10%	0%
— Parent survey	10%	0%

| — Teacher survey | 10% | 0% |
| — Outside audit | 20% | 0% |

| | -------- | |
| | 50% | |

Districts using this system have achieved more learning, confidence, morale, cost-effectiveness, teamwork, and accountability.

DESCRIPTIONS OF ADMINISTRATIVE EVALUATION COMPONENTS

Traditionally, superintendents protected and defended administrators, with hard data kept secret from board and public. (In return, administrators would defend and protect the superintendent.) This outline shows how the transition to more participative and results-oriented management can be positive and constructive. This plan links board and staff with positive evidence of responsibility and performance.

- It is the foundation for board and public confidence needed to support adequate funding of good schools and fair salaries.
- It answers the board's question of how to base administrative salaries on performance.
- It defines the leadership that the board, administrators, and teachers should expect from the superintendent.
- The board's role is to evaluate the superintendent: Has he or she completed each of these components?

Soft Data—Evaluation Process

The board should expect the superintendent to carry out this process and report results to them.

Analysis of results. Perhaps the best way to explain this analysis is with two examples:

- A new principal takes over a school that has proven somewhat difficult in years past because it is a little further from the center of town than other schools in the district, and the community has a tendency to be somewhat more fragmented. The new principal's major challenge in the current year, as a young woman replacing a senior veteran of 20 years, is to take charge successfully, especially in relationships with parents, teachers, and students.
- A new director of the physical education department in a high school is taking over from a husband-and-wife team who had not yet developed an equal distribution of opportunities between boys and girls, and who had allowed

some older faculty members to work a light schedule. The challenge is to modernize and turn around the department.

These circumstances faced by administrators must be understood by the superintendent, and of course by the person directly responsible, and then considered at the end of a year. Discussion is usually better than writing; frequent contact, dialogue, and observation are valuable.

Personal Assessment. A verbal and analytical approach is usually best, in a format of strengths and improvement opportunities. Obviously much depends on the style of the superintendent, and this is highly individual. Development opportunities and career planning should also be stressed.

Achievements Compared with Objectives. This is preferable to responsibilities versus achievements, since it focuses on current issues and priorities. However, it is not as useful as the first two categories, since objectives are often incomplete and unrealistic, and usually cannot express the kinds of circumstances described in the examples above.

Achievements Compared with Responsibilities. Obviously this needs to be considered, but generally it is not a very useful way to differentiate; most administrators fulfill their responsibilities, or they would not be retained.

Checklists. This traditional method of administrative evaluation in schools is not worth very much. Like the Boy Scout oath or the Ten Commandments, these lists are generally unobjectionable, but they are not usually related to the job at hand, nor are they useful in distinguishing levels of performance.

Hard Data—Performance Information

This new area of evaluation for school administrators is sometimes a little frightening. These data, however, provide the best possible basis for building confidence, improving performance, and convincing board and public that taxpayers are getting their money's worth. Every administrator and teacher winds up with a solid base of documentary information proving that a good job has been done.

• One important difference between the soft and hard portions of the evaluation is that the soft side is highly individualized to each administrator, whereas the hard side is oriented more to teamwork and group measures. Many administrative positions will have few direct measures of performance. But the management team as a whole is responsible for total district productivity: learning, confidence, morale, and cost-effectiveness. A useful contribution is made to teamwork and the willingness of administrators to help each other by such group measures.

• Another difference is that the soft side is very much influenced by the style and personality of the superintendent. The hard side is standardized in form and procedure—a useful balance.

Although the evaluation process and performance information are both important, from the board's point of view information is more visible and convincing. This is really the key to accountability—justifying fair teacher and administrator salaries by proving good performance. Performance information serves the same function as earnings, sales, and investment data in a business—proof that a good job is being done, so internal confidence and public funding can be maintained.

24

Board/Superintendent Evaluation: Criteria and Process

One of the most difficult board responsibilities is evaluation of the superintendent. In a healthy situation there is a great deal of confidence and dependence on the superintendent by the board, since he is a full-time professional chief executive, and they are part-time amateurs. Superintendents train and support their boards to make them look smart, even though the work of the district and support for the board are being provided by the staff. On the other hand, when some or all board members are not happy with the superintendent or are dissatisfied with the district's performance, the situation becomes more than a little awkward, and considerable diplomatic and managerial skills are required. Obviously this makes evaluation a delicate and difficult challenge at best. In spite of the inherent challenge of evaluating the superintendent, this is the board's greatest single point of leverage for improving school performance and management. If a board fails to persuade its superintendent of the desirability of moving in the direction of participative management and measuring results, and to hire a superintendent based on these criteria, then evaluation is not likely to be very effective.

Although there is a natural potential conflict of interest in representing both the community and the staff that can manifest itself at the board/superintendent interface, it is surprising how well this works in most situations. Usually this is because of the skill and integrity of the superintendent in balancing various, sometimes conflicting, interests and recommending an appropriate course of action to the board. Frankly, it is surprising, given the political arena in which superintendents operate, the high level of national concern about schools today, and the difficult transition from authority to participation and from secrecy to information, that superintendents are as successful as they are. I believe it is a tribute to the exceptionally high level of talent and dedication throughout education—from school bus drivers, cafeteria staff, and custodians through the vitally important school and central office secretaries, teachers and other professional staff and supporting aides, administrators in schools and at the central office, culminating (one hopes) in the talent at the superintendent's level, where the potential impact on and contribution to performance and management are greatest. I have had the opportunity to work with many industries in this country and abroad, and I have never found as talented and dedicated a group of people as I have in education in the United States.

The interface between the superintendent and board has not been altogether smooth, however, in many districts during recent years. If you think about the transition described in this book, I think you will see why this might be so. A historic shift from authority, often through a period of chaos and conflict (although sometimes avoiding this step), and finally reaching participative management and effectively utilized performance information is a tremendously difficult challenge. Industry had the luxury of accomplishing this over a much longer period of time than education has. No wonder superintendents complain about overinvolved boards, and boards about superintendents who are not as participative and communicative as they might like.

Following is a summary of the concept of governance, management, and performance translated into criteria for board and superintendent evaluation.

BOARD/SUPERINTENDENT EVALUATION—SUMMARY

One key point of leverage for the board in improving school performance and management is evaluation of the superintendent. These criteria are based on the school governance, management, and performance system that I have developed from 15 years of research and experience.

1. *Governance.* Board policies and behavior, and superintendent leadership; teamwork, accountability, performance, and management
   - Efficient, constructive board meetings
   - Information provided to the board
   - Recommended decisions
   - Leadership of board and staff

2. *Management.* A positive system linking board and staff through teamwork and accountability: planning, information, evaluation, and compensation

- Communication and teamwork
- Administrative evaluation and compensation based on performance
- Teacher development and evaluation that is fair, effective, and operational

3. *Performance.* Objective evidence to prove where a good job is being done and identify improvement opportunities: student learning, parent/teacher satisfaction, cost effectiveness
   - Test data analysis
   - Parent survey
   - Teacher survey
   - Outside audit

Governance

The first criterion is the overall governance of the district. You might be surprised to find the policies and behavior of the board, as well as superintendent leadership, included in a single category. My experience is that these are inseparable, and in this sense superintendent and board are operating as a single unit. If they are not, governance is not likely to be very effective.

Efficient and constructive board meetings will be a function of presidential leadership as well as of superintendent preparation. I have seen an extraordinary range from short, effective meetings even when dealing with difficult subjects to those running into the small hours of the morning. Sometimes a few difficult board members can make the situation almost impossible for the superintendent and for their colleagues on the board.

Information provided to the board should be concise and relevant, and give the board a sound basis for making decisions. Do not expect all of this information to be shared in public meetings. Some of it will bear upon personnel evaluations and, depending on the laws in your particular state, may not be allowed to be discussed in public meetings. Board discussion and debate of delicate issues in a committee format or in some way that does not involve just public positioning is usually important, although this can conflict with sunshine laws and the proper requirement for a board to hold most, if not all, of its discussions in public meetings, or at least with the public permitted to attend.

The superintendent's recommendations to the board should be sound and appropriate, even though the board may not necessarily always accept them. There is always room for questioning, challenging, discussion, and debate before final decisions are made on such important items as salaries, budgets, curriculum, and evaluation.

Finally, the superintendent's leadership of board and staff should be judged as perhaps the single most important factor.

Management

Under the second criterion is the management system detailed in Part VI of this book. Obviously the main factor is whether a positive system has been developed and implemented, linking board and staff through teamwork and accountability, with planning, information, evaluation, and compensation. This is likely to take a few years. As each district enters, goes through, and comes out of the transitional period, the board will need to be sensitive to appropriate levels of expectations. I see three specific categories in this area:

- Communication and teamwork in a general sense among board, staff, public, parents, and students
- Administrative evaluation and compensation based on performance using the system specified in Chapter 21
- Teacher development and evaluation that are fair, effective, and operational, not just the paper systems that many districts have.

There is a great deal of experimentation and creative development going on in these areas. They are subject to much improvement in practical value and the positive support given by districts to teachers through evaluation, development, and aggressive recruitment of the talent needed to get the job done.

There is also a small negative component: not all teachers continue to be effective every year, and there is some need for weeding out. In my experience this might amount to as little as 1 percent per year. It is vitally important that the board make sure its district administrators are doing this job, which is always unpleasant, and easier to avoid than to confront. If your administrators are not doing this, the accumulation of incompetent teachers over even a few years could seriously erode the performance of your district, and over many years could practically eliminate progress. I have seen individual schools that have literally fallen to student learning growth rates of zero, largely because of inadequate recruitment and evaluation of teachers.

Performance

The final category is performance, and the criterion here is objective evidence to prove where a good job is being done, and to identify improvement opportunities in the critically important categories of student learning, parent/teacher satisfaction, and cost-effectiveness. This should specifically include thorough, easy-to-understand presentations of results from the following:

- Test data analysis
- Parent surveys
- Teacher surveys
- Financial planning and cost analysis in general and in each of several major cost categories, such as buses, lunchrooms, buildings, staffing levels, and salaries

An outside audit is needed to confirm performance information and to assure consistency, comparisons, and credibility.

BOARD/SUPERINTENDENT EVALUATION PROCESS

Following is a summary of the process of evaluation that I have found most effective. This is a three-part process for board/superintendent evaluation that supports implementation of the governance-management-performance system.

1. *Personal Observations.* Naturally, board members have informal impressions of schools, board meetings, and superintendent support. There will also be telephone calls and other communication from parents and teachers. This anecdotal evidence—common-sense impressions of parents and staff communicated directly to the governing body—is unavoidable, and helps to tie school districts to their local community. There is obviously a risk of bias or narrow viewpoints.

2. *Management.* The board should assess planning, information, administrative evaluation and compensation based on performance, accountability, teacher development and evaluation in a way that constitutes fair, effective planning and use of performance information.

3. *Performance.* This is the most important aspect of the board's responsibility, comparable with sales, profits, and return on investment for a business. This must include test data analysis for multiple years that is accurate and comparable, as well as comparisons with patterns and trends in other districts, and parent/teacher surveys. Accuracy, credibility, and comparisons require an outside audit. This is the public service counterpart of what an industrial board of directors gets in an audited financial statement.

You might be surprised to find personal observations as the first category. Obviously this has the potential to be unfair and personal. However, my experience is that this is unavoidable, and not necessarily negative. Each board member will have, as a result of his or her personal experience, an impression of district performance that cannot be put aside, regardless of what other factors might be involved. This is an inherent risk of the superintendent's job, depending as it does on a board of part-time amateurs who change frequently.

The second part of the process should be assessment of the district's management systems. I suggest that you use Part VI of this book. As noted in Chapter 23, the superintendent should be reporting in some detail on results of the district's administrative and teacher evaluation plans, so you will have some firsthand insight into the operation and results of these systems. The board should not be evaluating administrators and teachers directly, but it should be seeing the results of these evaluation systems, so that it can judge whether the systems are working effectively, fairly, and with the right balance between staff and public interests.

The third category of the process is performance. The performance information specified in Part V of this book is what we consider to be most relevant: test data analysis for student learning, and parent/teacher surveys to identify perceptions and concerns. The credibility, experience, perspective, and comparisons available through an outside audit are essential—the public service counterpart of what an industrial board of directors gets in an audited financial statement.

Some boards like to use a specific checklist of criteria to evaluate the superintendent, while others prefer a more informal telephone survey, perhaps by the board president, of other members. In either case it is important that some kind of process exist and that feedback be provided to the superintendent as a result. You might want to vary the approach from year to year, depending on circumstances. If you have specific concerns that seem to imply a marked difference of opinions or direction between the superintendent and the board, then I would recommend a more thorough exploration of the situation—or getting a new superintendent who can meet the board's requirements. I do not mean to encourage more turnover of superintendents, but there are situations where boards simply have a point of view different from that of the leader; and in these circumstances there is no practical alternative to a new leader.

25

Standards for Performance and Management

This chapter contains standards for district performance and management. Criteria for success are specified, with questions and a checklist that you can use for assessing your own district. These criteria represent a wide range of districts from the very best to those still mired in conflict or the traditional authoritarian approach. You can use these criteria as a general conceptual framework, or the form can actually be filled in by school board members to provide a consensus view of strengths and weaknesses in your district's performance and management.

SUMMARY

These are recommended standards for good school performance and management with teamwork and accountability.

1. *Teachers satisfied and productive*
   - Involvement
   - Communication
   - Working conditions
   - Performance information
   - Informed
   - Staff development
   - Common goals with board
   - Selective recruitment
   - Fair evaluation
   - Reward for performance
   - Positive relationships

2. *Parents satisfied and appreciative*
   - Responsive to constituents
   - Parents surveyed
   - Cooperative relations
   - Taxpayers informed
   - Inquiries welcomed
   - Parents involved

3. *Students learning and developing*
   - Test data analyzed and used
   - Parent/teacher surveys
   - Student opinions
   - Performance goals
   - Positive experience
   - Appropriate curriculum

4. *Costs planned and controlled*
   - Sound financial planning
   - Costs controlled, analyzed
   - Performance information
   - Taxpayers satisfied
   - Support services cost-effective

5. *Board accountable and supportive*
   - Policy of management and performance
   - Good performance: student learning, parent and teacher satisfaction, cost-effectiveness
   - Confident, supportive, appreciative
   - Staff teamwork
   - Accountable, with information
   - Board delegates, not overinvolved
   - Meetings organized, short

6. *Management*
   - Communication, teamwork
   - Evaluation fair and effective
   - Information, outside audit
   - Sound recommendations to board
   - Board operations effective
   - Administrative responsibility.

DETAILS

Following are details of these school performance and management standards. High performance is on the left and low performance is on the right.

SCHOOL PERFORMANCE AND MANAGEMENT STANDARDS

HIGH	MIDDLE	LOW

Overall the District is Characterized by:

HIGH	MIDDLE	LOW
High performance relative to goals and resources; teamwork, pride and confidence.	Satisfactory performance relative to goals and resources; relationships of confusion, suspicion and concern.	Low performance relative to goals and resources; relationships of antagonism, bitterness and frustration.

I. TEACHERS

Satisfied and Productive

Principal Results

The Staff Is:

HIGH	MIDDLE	LOW
Satisfied, involved, evaluated, treated fairly, performing well; morale high.	Uneasy, uninvolved, evaluated but not effectively, sometimes treated fairly, not performing as well as they might; morale unsettled.	Frustrated, alienated unevaluated, demoralized, performing poorly.

Supporting Policies and Practices

	HIGH	MIDDLE	LOW
1.	Teachers involved in decision-making.	Teachers involved in some decision-making but an uneasy feeling of antagonism exists between teachers and management and board.	Teachers not involved in decision-making
2.	Superintendent meets with staff regularly.	Superintendent meets with staff occasionally but usually through union channels.	Superintendent meets with staff only through union channels.

3.	Staff has superior working conditions and appear content.	Staff has reasonable working conditions but feel they are taken advantage of.	Staff working conditions are a regular source of friction.
4.	Staff informed of personal and district performance.	Some district and personal performance data collected but not shared with staff.	No personal or district performance data collected.
5.	Staff informed of board and management actions.	Staff finds out about board actions from union or local press.	Staff not informed of management or board decisions.
6.	Staff development program is organized, preplanned, funded and based on program and individual teacher needs.	Staff development occurs occasionally, but is not planned, individualized or or adequately funded.	No staff development program.
7.	Staff/management/ board are aware of goals and satisfied with process of goal development.	Staff/management/ board have some common goals and interests but are rather wary of each other.	Staff/management/ board do not have common goals and have an adversarial relationship.
8.	Staff selection practices involve high standards; many candidates interviewed and best person selected for jobs.	Staff selected from unsolicited applications.	Staff assigned to schools without regard to teacher or principal choice.
9.	Teacher evaluation fair and effective, based on information, feedback and results.	Teacher evaluation not based on information, feedback and results.	No teacher evaluation.

10.	Teachers rewarded for good performance in recognition and compensation.	Good teaching performance recognized but not rewarded.	Good teaching performance neither recognized nor rewarded.
11.	Good board/staff/ management relations; no need for employees union.	Teacher union recognized but contract covers only wages and other benefits.	Union recognized, ironclad contract hampers board/ management.

II. PARENTS

Satisfied and Appreciative

Principal Results

Parents and Community are:

Satisfied, involved and confident of district performance.	Suspicious; concerned, unclear about district performance.	Complaining, irate, dissatisfied with the district.

Supporting Policies and Practices

12.	Students, parents and taxpayers viewed as consumers of district programs.	Parents and taxpayers viewed as necessary but not taken seriously.	Parents and taxpayers are viewed as complainers and ignored.
13.	Parents surveyed on key issues.	Parents occasionally asked for feedback.	Parents not asked for input.
14.	Board, parents and staff work together.	Board, parents and staff view themselves as groups will different purposes.	Board, parents and staff are adversaries.
15.	Taxpayers kept informed on school activities, finances, programs through multiple channels.	Taxpayers informed only by local press on district activities.	Taxpayers seldom informed by anyone on status of the district.

16.	Parent inquiries, criticisms and suggestions are welcomed.	Parent inquiries, criticisms and suggestions are tolerated.	Parent inquiries, criticisms and suggestions are discouraged.
17.	A large number of parent volunteers working with schools.	Some parent volunteers working in schools but not well organized.	No parent volunteers in schools.

III. STUDENTS

Learning and Developing

Principal Results

Students are:

Learning as a group and individually in keeping with their ability.	No one knows how well students are actually progressing from year to year.	Test scores, dropout and attendance rates are on the decline.

Supporting Policies and Practices

18.	Test data analyzed and used to improve district performance.	Test data available but not analyzed and used for improvement of instruction or programs.	Test data is collected but not used.
19.	Community feedback is used to improve district performance.	Community feedback not regularly gathered or used to improve programs.	Community feedback is not gathered.
20.	A teacher evaluation system identifies strengths and weeknesses.	A teacher evaluation checklist is used.	No teacher evaluation system.
21.	Management evaluation system is based on goals achieved.	A management evaluation form is used.	No management evaluation system.

22. | The board looks yearly at district performance in terms of pre-determined goals. | The board assumes district performance is good, but does not have information to back up the claim. | The board never looks at district performance. |

IV. COSTS

Planned and Controlled

Principal Results

Costs are:

| Kept at a minimum in terms of district educational production. | No one knows what costs per building or service are or how they compare with other districts. | No attempt made to provide cost analysis information for public and board. |

Supporting Policies and Practices

23. | Definite attempts are made to relate educational productivity to cost. | Educational productivity is not looked at; costs are assumed to rise. | No attempt to look at educational productivity or minimize costs. |

24. | Cost effectiveness of program is analyzed. | Cost effectiveness of program is assumed. | Cost effectiveness of program is never considered. |

25. | Program costs are at or below comparable districts. | Program costs are at or above comparable districts. | Program costs are not compared to comparable districts. |

V. BOARD

Accountable and Supportive

<u>Principal Results</u>

<u>Board and Management are:</u>

Well organized and effective, working as a team to achieve results shown above.	Unclear of responsibilities, capable of achieving results but not doing	Adversarial and antagonistic, failing to achieve results and unable to do so.

<u>Supporting Policies and Practices</u>

26.	Adheres to its role of determining purpose, goals, policy and evaluating results.	Sometimes delves into administration and/or fails to monitor results.	Often involved in all aspects of school operation or not involved at all.
27.	Membership is stable and the members are consistently trying to improve their performance individually and as a group.	Membership has some turnover but little effort made on individual or group performance improvement.	Membership turnover is rapid and no effort made to improve performance.
28.	Meetings are brief, organized, thorough and businesslike with members coming to meetings prepared.	Meetings are long and many members have not previously studied the agenda and supporting material.	Meetings are unorganized, long and confusing. Members pay little attention to agenda or supporting material.
29.	Members concentrate on evaluation of district program results.	Assumes district is achieving results, but lacks evidence.	Information on district performance is based on personal experience and an occasional telephone call or incidental conversation.

VI. MANAGEMENT

Responsible and Competent

Principal Results

Management is:

Well organized and effective, working as a team to achieve results shown above.	Unclear of responsibilities, capable of achieving results but not doing so.	Adversarial and antagonistic, failing to achieve results and unable to do so.

Supporting Policies and Practices

30.	Understands and implements Board goals.	Assumes it knows Board goals and is implementing them.	Does not have written Board goals and is unsure of what is expected.
31.	Evaluated on effectiveness of program performance in terms of goals.	Assumed to be doing a good job but no evidence exists related to goals.	Not evaluated objectively on performance because no goals exist.
32.	Compensated fairly, separately from teaching staff, and based on performance and job market comparisons.	Compensated, but not based on performance or job market comparisons.	Salary paid below job market comparisons, not based on performance and decisions are made far into the school year.
33.	Has sufficient number of administrators.	Has done no analysis of administrator needs.	Has not enough administrators, or too many.
34.	Has clearly defined organization and responsibilities with necessary authority.	Has no written responsibilities, lacks organization and authority.	Responsibilities not defined or organized to achieve Board goals.

26

Results: Learning, Confidence, and Morale

This chapter presents a summary of research results documenting performance improvements. Descriptions of background and performance in each of the ten research districts are summarized briefly. These districts include a representative sample of upscale and middle-class suburbs, as well as urban communities and rural areas. Their achievement—37 percent more learning, plus more parent/teacher satisfaction, board confidence, teamwork, accountability, and cost-effectiveness—is indicative of the improvements that American schools could make if the board policies, management plans, and performance measures described in this book were more widely applied.

Like the four-minute mile, or statistics on aging or running, historical standards of school performance have undershot human capability. Pilot districts in our research on school performance and management have achieved positive and important results:

- Three years of learning are being added to eight years of school.
- Even greater improvements are being achieved in urban communities.
- Teachers do make a difference.

These findings have obvious importance for civil rights, economic competitiveness, and urban renewal. This is the foundation we need for America's future progress and success, to be competitive in the world economy, and to realize equal opportunity for all our citizens.

These three common assumptions are slowing America's progress:

- Students and teachers are doing about as well as can be expected.
- Students in cities (mostly black) cannot do very well in school.
- Teachers do not make much difference (after income, education, and family circumstances are considered).

These assumptions are discouraging. They are negative. They have kept us from trying harder and from achieving more. And they are false.

Management research and experience has led to these findings:

- America's students and teachers can succeed at levels much higher than those currently being accomplished: for example, adding three years of learning to eight years of school.
- Even more dramatic improvements can be achieved by students in urban communities: three examples have doubled student learning.
- Teachers do make a difference—from growth rates of as little as zero to as much as two years per year in school.

These findings show how we can build on America's past achievements in national democracy, agricultural productivity, and industrial efficiency—to meet today's requirements for effective schools and quality public services—with participative and results-oriented governance, management, and performance.

My conclusions are the following:

1. *America's Students and Teachers Can Achieve More Than Has Generally Been Assumed.*
   - Ten pilot districts where performance has been measured through outside audits for 10 to 15 years have added thirty-seven percent to student learning. They are achieving three more years of growth during eight years of school. This gives students a 3-year head start over the students in these same districts in earlier years.
   - Urban communities like Zion, North Chicago, and Hazel Crest have been able to double student learning, in effect adding four years of growth to eight years in school. This would seem to indicate the possible improvement opportunities available in America's cities.
   - Middle-class communities like Antioch have been able to add three years of growth to eight years in school.
   - Middle-class and upscale suburbs such as Lake Forest and Lombard have added two years of growth to eight years in school.
   - These improvements are based on analysis of growth rates, percentiles of achievement versus ability, and grade equivalent scores on all of the major national standardized achievement tests.
   - The resulting improvements in cost-effectiveness are giving taxpayers a 37

percent greater return on their investment. Satisfaction, confidence, morale, and teamwork have improved.

- Participating districts include a representative sample of urban, suburban, and rural communities.
- Because of the accelerated progress of their students in basic skills, several of these districts have been able to add subjects like foreign languages and algebra, for students capable of this work, in junior high rather than in high school.
- The advanced placement program is demonstrating that some high school students can function successfully in college-level courses.

2. *The Biggest Learning Gains Have Occurred in Urban Communities.*

- Contrary to common assumptions, very substantial performance improvements can be, and have been, achieved in urban communities.
- Three urban communities with high levels of poverty and minority students have doubled learning growth rates from 6 to 12 months per year (Zion, North Chicago, and Hazel Crest).
- Substantial improvements have been achieved in upscale and middle-class suburbs and rural communities such as Lake Forest, Antioch, Lake Villa, Ridgeland, Keeneyville, and Lombard.
- Other communities analyzed include Berwyn, Blue Island, Round Lake, Benjamin, Burr Ridge, Highwood-Highland Park, Lake Bluff, Big Hollow, Elmwood, and Waukegan.
- Districts in other states include Williamsburg, Virginia; Apache Junction, Arizona; Holland, Michigan; Lancaster, Wisconsin; and Merrillville, Indiana.

3. *Good Teaching Makes a Big Difference.*

- Some academic research on the correlation between achievement scores and factors such as family income, education, and economic circumstances has concluded that teachers do not make much difference.
- Our research, on the contrary, by measuring growth rates over a long period of time, indicates that good teaching and good schools do make a very substantial difference in student learning.
- Twice as much learning is occurring in well-managed, high-performance districts as in poorly managed, low-performance ones—even in the same communities.
- We see performance ranges from as low as zero growth to as high as two years of growth for a year in school. This seems to be a realistic range of performance and a measure of the impact of good teaching.
- Taxpayers who have long felt there is a difference between schools, and as a consequence wonder whether they are getting their money's worth from their investment in taxes, seem to be right. Here is objective data showing a wide range of performance.
- Some high-performance districts are not high-expenditure districts. Some

of the best performance and improvements have been achieved by the poorest districts in their respective counties, such as Keeneyville in Du-Page County and North Chicago in Lake County (Chicago metropolitan area).

4. *Performance Differences Are Driven by Participative Management and Performance Measures.*

- The key factor in these performance improvements does not seem to be textbooks, curriculum, facilities, or structure, but how the district is managed at three levels: board policies, participative management, and performance measures.

- Focusing on the school's mission of student learning, expecting a year's growth for a year in school, measuring results, and reporting back to teachers and principals so that they can take appropriate action, in a climate of participative management and positive support, are the key factors in improvement.

5. These Findings Have Important and Positive Implications for America's Future Progress and Success.

- Whether these performance improvements could be replicated across the country could be discovered only by wider application. If all of them, even some substantial part, could be replicated, this would provide the foundation we need for America's future national progress and success.

- If students in urban communities can perform at the levels indicated by our research, then there is no reason to tolerate the poor performance of many of America's urban schools today.

- This would be a more promising solution to America's urban problems than more prisons, welfare, deficits, or federal troops.

- Reducing or eliminating the underclass and getting America's civil rights progress moving forward again would be positive benefits of moving in this direction.

- America's economic competitiveness would be materially supported by the addition of three years of learning to eight years in school.

- The cost of social services and prisons, criminal justice, welfare, and unemployment would be reduced. Pressures for spending on these services beyond what we can afford are causing America's federal deficit; this problem, too, might be aided by improved school effectiveness.

- The most important benefits of good schools are the human values to students in the success, achievement, satisfaction, fulfillment, and contribution of their lives.

- America's future economic success and social progress now depend primarily on improvements in the productivity of public services, building on our past success in national democracy, agricultural productivity, and industrial efficiency. This fourth phase of the American revolution will be as important for our future as the three earlier phases of industry, agriculture, and democracy were for our history.

• The concept of participative and results-oriented management can achieve similar productivity improvements in other public services, such as local government. Changes in the authoritarian and bureaucratic approach exemplified by America's criminal justice and social service systems could permit even greater improvements, on a scale equaling America's earlier accomplishments in agricultural efficiency and industrial productivity.

These results, adding three years of learning to eight years in school, the foundation we need for future progress and success, will enable America to compete successfully in a world economy and to realize equal opportunity for all our citizens.

PERFORMANCE IMPROVEMENTS IN TEN DISTRICTS

These districts improved student learning by an average of 37 percent while raising parent/teacher satisfaction, board confidence, teamwork, accountability, and cost-effectiveness.

1.	Zion	100%	
2.	Lake Forest	20%	
3.	North Chicago	50%	(100% in junior high school)
4.	Antioch	30%	
5.	Lake Villa	20%	
6.	Lombard	20%	
7.	Keeneyville	30%	(100% in junior high school)
8.	Benjamin	10%	
9.	Hazel Crest	40%	
10.	Ridgeland	30%	

Following are summaries of results in the ten districts that provided the original management and performance research underlying this book. These results were originally published in *Quality School Results* (vol. 12 of the School Management Model series). Summaries of community character and results in each district are included in *Measure Your School* (vol. 1 of the School Board Accountability series).

Zion District #6

Zion is in the northeastern corner of Illinois, on Lake Michigan, immediately south of Wisconsin. Founded in the nineteenth century as a religious utopia, the community is working class and racially mixed. It has a fine city plan, in the shape of a flag, with open space, parks, recreational facilities, and parkways. Since 1973 District #6 has approximately doubled the amount of student learning. The net effect is a proportional increase in cost-effectiveness and value received by taxpayers for their investment in community schools. For example, average annual growth from 1973 to 1986 doubled from 6 to 12 months annually.

Lake Forest District #67

Lake Forest is an affluent suburb north of Chicago. In 1971 a new superintendent inherited a controversial school closing, a defeated referendum, the need for immediate budget cuts of 25 percent, and early retirement of the previous superintendent. Gradual increases have occurred in student learning in virtually every subject and grade. Several high school-level courses have been moved down to the junior high school, such as foreign language and advanced math; more is being accomplished in less time.

North Chicago District #64

North Chicago is a working-class community in the industrial strip along Lake Michigan that begins north of the Chicago suburbs and runs with some interruptions through Milwaukee. The problems of smokestack industries are evident in closed stores and factories. Student learning has shown dramatic improvement since 1980. Average annual growth increased by 71 percent in reading and 43 percent in math. A special feature has been reorganization to put seventh and eighth grade students into elementary buildings instead of a junior high school.

Antioch District #34

Antioch is a small town in the Illinois lake district bordering Wisconsin. These exerpts from the outside audit report summarize results:

- A remarkable improvement in student learning has been achieved.
  —Composite percentiles increased from 55 percent to 69 percent for the eighth grade.
  —Grade equivalents increased from 9.6 to 11.0 for the eighth grade.
  —Annual growth of 14 to 16 months per year compares with a national average of 10.
- Improvements have occurred in virtually all subjects and grades.
- Strong learning growth seems to be pushing up educational ability scores.

Lake Villa District #41

Lake Villa, in West Lake County, south of Antioch, serves two distinctly different communities. This district has had an exceptionally strong pattern of performance improvement since 1976.

- Percentiles of achievement have increased dramatically—for example, from 18 to 81 at the eighth grade level.
- Grade level achievements have gone up sharply—for example, from 8.0 to 9.5 for the eighth grade.

Lombard District #44

Lombard is one of the older suburbs in Dupage County, with a mix of expensive new homes and older, somewhat deteriorating neighborhoods subject to the fringes of inner city problems. District #44 has achieved strong performance and significant improvement during the past few years:

- Increasing average annual growth by 20 percent to 25 percent since 1976—from 11–12 months to 13–15 months.
- Increasing percentiles of achievement and grade equivalents with a rising pattern through the years and grade levels. For example, the eighth grade achieved 11.8 in 1986 compared with 10.9 in 1985 (grade equivalent).

Keeneyville District #20

Keeneyville is west and north of Lombard, a newer community consisting of two suburban developments east and west of a rural intersection that was the site of Mr. Keeney's vegetable farm. Considerable improvement has been made in student achievement since 1975, especially in the junior high school.

- The overall student learning growth rate of 11 months per year (compared with a national average of 10) is being achieved in every subject and grade.
- These growth rates are considerably improved from 1976, when district growth averaged only eight months per year per student. At the junior high school level, learning growth has approximately doubled.
- Composite percentile scores in the early years were averaging in the 50s and in recent years in the 80s.

Benjamin District #25

Benjamin is further west in DuPage County, an area that has grown rapidly and will continue to do so. District #25 has maintained its record of good performance and improvement.

- Continued strengthening of performance is occurring in the seventh grade, which appeared to be a weakness several years ago.

- There are good growth rates in all areas, averaging 11 months per year, compared with a national average of 10.
- Percentiles of achievement continue to be high, mostly in the 90s, leaving only limited room for further improvement.

Hazel Crest District #152 1/2

Hazel Crest District #152 1/2 straddles a traditional racial boundary south of Chicago in a district about half black and half white. These are highlights of conclusions reached in the 1980 test score analysis:

- District #152 1/2 has improved from below national averages in annual growth for reading and math to above these averages in 1979—improving from 8 months to 10 months of growth annually for reading and from 8 to 12 months of growth annually for math from 1974/1975 to 1978/1979.
- Average annual growth has improved in every grade and every school for both reading and math during this period.

Ridgeland District #122

Ridgeland District #122 serves the Oak Lawn suburban area southwest of Chicago. The long-serving superintendent has an unusually high interest in school management and performance and has been willing to pioneer in leadership in this direction. District #122 has had a strong pattern of performance and improvement.

- Percentiles of achievement have improved, shifting from a declining pattern through the grades to one that is level and perhaps slightly improving.
- Substantial improvements have been made in grade level achievements.
- Annual growth rates were particularly strong in the early 1980s, an average of about 13 months per year.

Bibliography

The following books and articles include the reading list prepared for my school management case study course at Northwestern University's School of Education and Social Policy and Graduate School of Management. To that list, originally published in *Improving School Performance* (Praeger, 1983), I have added books and articles on the origins of school management, school reform, and general management, and handbooks on implementation.

CHANGES IN THE ORGANIZATION OF EDUCATION, CONTENT OF PROGRAMS, AND RESPONSES TO ACCOUNTABILITY DEMANDS

Cresswell, M., Murphy, M., and Kerchner, C. *Teachers' Unions and Collective Bargaining.* Berkeley, CA: McCutchan, 1980.

Erickson, D. A., and Reller, T. L., Editors. *The Principal in Metropolitan Schools.* Berkeley, CA: McCutchan, 1979.

Harnischfeger, A. "Curricular control and learning time: District policy, teacher strategy and pupil choice." *Educational Evaluation and Policy Analysis* 2 (November–December 1980):19.

Lutz, F., and Iannoccone, L., Editors. *Public Participation in Local School Districts.* Lexington, MA: Lexington Books, 1978.

Millman J., Editor. *Handbook of Teacher Evaluation.* Beverly Hills, CA: Sage, 1981.

CHANGES IN THE EXTERNAL ENVIRONMENT IMPACTING ON THE EDUCATIONAL SYSTEM AND POLICY

Kirst, M. "The changing politics of education: Actions and strategies." In *The Changing Politics of Education*, edited by E. K. Mosher and J. L. Wagoner, Jr., pp. 145–170. Berkeley, CA: McCutchan, 1976.

Rubin, L., Editor. *Critical Issues in Educational Policy: An Administrator's Overview*. Boston: Allyn and Bacon, 1980.

Thurston, P. "Is good law good education?" In *Review of Research in Education*, edited by D. Berliner. Washington, D.C.: American Educational Research Association, 1980.

Timpane, J., Editor. *The Federal Interest in the Financing of Schooling*. Cambridge, MA: Ballinger, 1978.

Wise, A. E. *Legislated Learning*. Berkeley: University of California Press, 1979.

THE GOALS OF SCHOOLING—DIVERSIFICATION AND CHANGES

Atkin, J. M. "The government in the classroom." *Daedalus: Journal of the American Academy of Arts and Sciences* (Summer 1980):85–97.

Fiorian, M. P. "The decline of collective responsibility in American politics." *Daedalus: Journal of the American Academy of Arts and Sciences* (Summer 1980):25–45.

Firestone, W. A. "Images of schools and patterns of change." *American Journal of Education* 8 (August 1980):459–487.

Graham, P. A. "Whither equality of educational opportunity." *Daedalus: Journal of the American Academy of Arts and Sciences* (Summer 1980):115–132.

Lightfoot, S. L. *Worlds Apart: Relationships Between Families and Schools*. New York: Basic Books, 1978.

Wood, R. "The disassembling of American education." *Daedalus: Journal of the American Academy of Arts and Sciences* (Summer 1980):99–113.

SCHOOL PERFORMANCE

Copperman, Paul. *The Literacy Hoax: the Decline of Reading, Writing and Learning in the Public Schools and What We Can Do About It*. New York: William Morrow, 1978.

"Help! Teacher can't teach: The multi-faceted crisis of American public schools." *Time*, June 16, 1980, pp. 54–63.

"Kappan special section on teacher education." *Phi Delta Kappan* 63 (October 1981):106–133.

Kozol, Jonathan. *Death at an Early Age: The Destruction of the Hearts and Minds of Negro Children in the Boston Public Schools*. Boston: Houghton, Mifflin, 1967.

Mitchell, Richard. *Less Than Words Can Say*. Boston: Little, Brown, 1979.

Phi Delta Kappan 63 (December 1981). Special issue on collective bargaining.

"The plight of U.S. secondary education: Why are today's high school students learning less and disliking it more?" *Time*, November 14, 1977, pp. 62–75.

Rutter, M. Maughan, B., Mortimore, P., and Ouston, J. *Fifteen Thousand Hours*. Cambridge, MA: Harvard University Press, 1979.

"The 13th annual Gallup poll of the public's attitudes toward the public schools." *Phi Delta Kappan* 62 (September 1981):33.

SCHOOL MANAGEMENT

Allen, J. L., and Genck, F. H. "Management education: The school of management concept." *American Assembly of Collegiate Schools of Business Bulletin* 6 (April 1970).

Genck, F. H. "Public management in America." *American Assembly of Collegiate Schools of Business Bulletin* 9 (April 1973): 1–13.

———. "The school board's role." Presentation to the 1980 National School Boards Association Convention, San Francisco, May 1980.

———. "Improving performance." *The School Administrator* 39 (January 1982):14–15.

———. "Make your school system accountable." *The American School Board Journal* 169 (February 1982):34.

———. *Northwestern School Management Course Case Study Book* (Fredric H. Genck, 1982).

———. *Improving School Performance.* New York: Praeger, 1983.

Genck, F. H., and Hay, D. W. "Local government reorganization in England." *Local Government Chronicle*, July 17, 24, 31, and August 7, 1971.

Genck, F. H., and Klingenberg, A. J. *Effective Schools Through Effective Management.* Springfield: Illinois Association of School Boards, 1978.

ORIGINS OF SCHOOL MANAGEMENT

Dewey, John. *Democracy and Education.* New York: Macmillan, 1916.

James, William. *Pragmatism.* New York: Meridan Books, 1955.

Scott, Walter Dill. *Personnel Management.* New York: McGraw-Hill, 1961.

SCHOOL REFORM

Bloom, Alan. *Closing of the American Mind.* New York: Touch-Tone Books, 1988.

Genck, F. H. "Making your system accountable." *American School Board Journal*, February 1982.

———. "Yes, merit pay can be horror but a few school systems have done it right." *American School Board Journal*, September 1983.

———. "Better schools through better management." *The School Administrator*, March 1984.

———. "Why you're not ready for merit pay yet." *The School Administrator*, September 1985.

———. "Why merit pay can succeed." *School Board News*, October 1985.

———. "What makes some schools better than others." *Illinois School Board Journal*, March/April 1986.

———. "How to improve school performance in your district." *The School Administrator*, August 1987.

———. "Measuring school performance." *American School Board Journal*, August 1989.

Grant, Gerald. *The World We Created at Hamilton High.* Cambridge, MA: Harvard University Press, 1988.

Hirsch, E. D., Jr. *Cultural Literacy, "What Every American Needs to Know."* New York: Random House, 1987.

Lortie, Dan. *Schoolteacher: A Sociological Study.* Chicago: University of Chicago Press, 1975.

GENERAL MANAGEMENT

Andrews, Kenneth. *The Concept of Corporate Strategy.* Homewood, IL: Dow Jones-Irwin, 1971.

Blanchard, Kenneth, and Johnson, Spencer. *One Minute Manager.* New York: Morrow, 1982.

Kantor, Rosabeth Moss. *The Change Masters.* New York: Simon and Schuster, 1983.

Porter, Michael E. *Competitive Strategy.* New York: Free Press–Macmillan, 1980.

IMPLEMENTATION HANDBOOKS

Genck, F. H. School Management Model series. Chicago: Institute for Public Management, 1984–1988.

1. *School Management Model*
2. *Administrative Evaluation and Compensation*
3. *Teacher Evaluation and Development*
4. *Planning and Communication*
5. *Test Data Analysis*
6. *Parent/Teacher Surveys*
7. *Financial Planning*
8. *Teacher Merit Pay*
9. *High School Management*
10. *Board Policy Summary*
11. *Self-Study Guide*
12. *Quality School Results*

————. School Board Accountability series. Chicago: Institute for Public Management, 1989.

1. *Measure Your School*
2. *Reward Your Staff*
3. *Evaluate Your Superintendent*

These detailed implementation handbooks and case studies are available from the Institute for Public Management, 550 W. Jackson Blvd., Chicago, IL 60661.

Index

ABOUT THE AUTHOR

FREDRIC H. GENCK is Managing Director of the Institute for Public Management in Chicago. He is the author of several books, including *Improving School Performance* (Praeger, 1983) and *Effective Schools Through Effective Management* (1978).